TAIWAN:

THE THREATENED DEMOCRACY

TAIWAN:

THE THREATENED DEMOCRACY

BRUCE HERSCHENSOHN

World Ahead Publishing, Inc.

Published by World Ahead Publishing, Inc., Los Angeles, CA

Copyright © 2006 by World Ahead Publishing, Inc.

World Ahead Publishing's books are available at special discounts for bulk purchases. World Ahead Publishing also publishes books in electronic formats. For more information, visit www.worldahead.com.

First Edition

ISBN 13-Digit 978-0-9778984-2-8
ISBN 10-Digit 0-9778984-2-3
LCCN 2006933774

Printed in the United States of America

10 9 8 7 6 5 4 3 2 1

CONTENTS

Dedicated to those Taiwanese who built their magnificent democracy, and who have the courage to reject anything short of living in liberty as a free and independent nation.

PREFACE

THIS BOOK is admittedly biased in support of liberty.

It was 1964 when I first visited Taiwan. My most recent trip was in December of 2005. Between those forty-one years were a host of trips to Taiwan as political events changed in the United States and in Taiwan. Through the years, all discussions with those I spoke to in Taiwan were valuable, providing differing views. Because the more recent events are particularly important in looking ahead, the following is a list of some of those in Taiwan with whom I discussed political events during the most recent visits to Taiwan:

Madam Annette Lu Hsiu-lien, Vice President of the Republic of China / Taiwan (Democratic Progressive Party).

Mayor Ma Ying-jeou, Chairman of the Kuomintang Party and Mayor of Taipei.

Mr. Jason Liao, Secretary General of the People First Party.

Mr. Chin-chiang Shu, Chairman of the Taiwan Solidarity Union Party.

Dr. Chong-pin Lin, Graduate Institute of International Affairs and Strategic Studies, Tamkang University.

Mr. Victor J. Chin, Director General of North American Affairs, Ministry of Foreign Affairs.

Dr. Hsin-huang Michael Hsio, National Policy Advisor to the President of the Republic of China / Taiwan.

Dr. David S. Hong, Vice President of the Taiwan Institute of Economic Research.

Mr. Li-pei Wu, Senior Advisor to the President of the Republic of China / Taiwan.

Mr. Yi-jen Chiu, Secretary General of the National Security Council.

Dr. Cheng-yi Lin, Director of the Institute of International Relations.

Mr. James Hsin-hua, Deputy Director General, Bureau of Foreign Trade, Ministry of Economic Affairs.

Dr. David Wei-feng Huang, Vice Chairman of Mainland Affairs Council, Executive Yuan.

Mr. T. K. Lee, Director of the Information and Liaison Office of the Government Information Office.

Mr. William J. T. Yih, Deputy Minister of the Government Information Office.

Mr. Chin-cheng Lo, Executive Director, Institute for National Policy Research.

Dr. I-chung Lai, Director of Foreign Policy Studies.

During those forty-one years, there were also countless discussions and forums regarding Taiwan at home in the United States. The names are too many to mention, and in some cases even remember, but beyond a doubt the most important were U.S. Congressman Dr. Walter Judd, Dr. K. C. Chen of the Formosan Association for Public Affairs and, of course, U.S. President Richard Nixon.

This is the story of U.S. policy regarding Taiwan as well as the People's Republic of China's policy regarding Taiwan, and the past, current, and possible future of the people of Taiwan.

Most historical events are covered through mid-2006. For consistency, all references to currency have been converted into U.S. dollars.

Bruce Herschensohn

A VITAL GLOSSARY IN ADVANCE

A GLOSSARY, if there is one, traditionally follows the major text of a book rather than preceding that text. But in the case of writing or reading about Taiwan and China a glossary *following* a text is too late. That's because China, Zhounghua, Red China, Mainland China, Communist China, and the People's Republic of China (PRC), are all used to describe the same entity. Moreover, Taiwan, Formosa, Ilha Formosa, Free China, Nationalist China, the Republic of China (ROC), and the Republic of China on Taiwan are all used to identify the island ninety-five miles east of China across the Taiwan Strait.

It should also be known that China was called the *Republic* of China from October 10, 1911, through September 30, 1949, and called the *People's* Republic of China from October 1, 1949, forward; each of the two names represent two entirely different governments, flags, and systems.

To further confuse all of this is that on January 1, 1979, the People's Republic of China introduced what it called the *Pinyin* system of pronouncing and spelling Chinese names for languages using the Roman alphabet. Suddenly, what was once called *Peiping* then *Peking* became *Beijing*, *Canton* became *Guangzhou*, and the map of China was filled with new spellings and pronunciations. The names of Chinese people were affected as well: *Mao Tse-tung* became *Mao Zedong*, *Chou En-lai* became *Zhou Enlai*, and *Teng Hsiao-ping* became *Deng Xiaoping*.

All of this has frustrated those speaking on the subject from students, analysts, and writers to presidents, kings, and prime ministers. Diplomats, at times, have fun with all this, since one name used or not used can be a subtle advocacy of a political position. A seemingly innocent use of terminology has the potential of advancing or subverting a policy.

The terms *Taipei* and *Beijing* are often used to describe the two political entities since those names are not under dispute. Both sides agree that Taipei is the capital of Taiwan (the capital of a nation or the capital of a province, depending on the person's political view) and Beijing is known by both sides as the current capital, current spelling, and current pronunciation of the capital city of the People's Republic of China. (Those two cities are often used just as Washington, D.C., is often used instead of saying "the government of the United States of America.")

For purposes of clarity, an attempt is made in this book to use the term or terms that are appropriate for the particular subjects and times being discussed with precedence given to the terms *Taiwan* and the *People's Republic of China*. The attempt, not always successful, is meant to give some degree of consistency and quick understanding.

CHAPTER ONE

THE QUEST AND THE ANTI-QUEST

THE DAY WAS COLD, the crowds were massive, and most national office-holders and appointees were there. All of that was traditional and customary for a U.S. President's Inauguration Day in Washington, D.C. What was not traditional or customary were the ten thousand troops, the closure of most streets, the security stations with metal detectors and hand-searching officers, and the fighter aircraft and helicopters patrolling the skies above the District of Columbia. It was to be the second-term inaugural of President George W. Bush and the first presidential inauguration since the September 11, 2001, attack on the United States of America.

That wasn't all that was unusual. President George W. Bush's second inaugural address of January 20, 2005, was beyond tradition and custom in the president's declaration of the most magnificent quest ever proclaimed by a leader of any nation: the liberty of every person in the world. "It is the policy of the United States to seek and support the growth of democratic movements and institutions in every nation and culture with the ultimate goal of ending tyranny in our world...We are ready for the greatest achievements in the history of freedom."

Dictators, authoritarians, tyrants, totalitarians, and terrorists did not concur with the pursuit proclaimed in President Bush's second inaugural address. And neither did many U.S. foreign service officers at the State Department, who winced at his words. After all, they were diplomats so they knew what to say.

"I thought his speech was great," they lied.
"Did he get that cleared by the Secretary?"

"I doubt it."

"Now what?"

"Don't panic."

"I'm not panicking. He's just not—he's just not—"

"I know."

"He's just not—like us. He just doesn't know."

"I know."

"So now what?"

There was a long silence, followed by a smile. *"China! That's what."*

There was another silence and then a sudden *"Of course! China!"*

"Do you know what I mean?"

"Not exactly."

"How does China integrate into a world of democracies? How can he explain that one? That can turn his whole quest into a fatal boomerang! Then, all by itself, things will be back to stability rather than his inexperienced dreaming."

Those dialogues of foreign service officers are not meant to be actual—but they are also not woven from offhand or casual imagination. They are meant to be an accurate reflection of the feelings of some major State Department foreign service officers on that day.

China has long been on the horizon of U.S. foreign policy. In the past it has sometimes been above the horizon and it has sometimes been simmering below the horizon, but China has expanded into constant visibility since it has become more than a potential superpower in military and economic strength. Its prominence in both fields has been enhanced by investment and trade with those in free countries including the United States. One other element has kept China above the horizon: its sustained obsession to own and extinguish the democracy of Taiwan.

Foreign service officers at the U.S. State Department wouldn't put it in these words, at least not publicly, but through the years many of them believed Taiwan to be expendable. The State Department, after all, had a philosophy far different than most presidents the department was meant to serve. Like other giant bureaucracies in the District of Columbia, many of those who worked for the State Department believed they were part of the permanent executive branch of the United States while presidents were temporary annoyances. Moreover, they felt it was their job, as careerists, not to advise a president, but to provide the president and his appointees with an education. The bureaucracy of careerists worked on all new presidential appointees as soon as they arrived at the department in which they were to serve, and often the bureaucracy succeeded in short time. Their mission was to see to it that the appointee would represent the careerist's policies to the president rather than the appointee representing the president's policies to the careerists.

The department didn't agree with President John F. Kennedy in 1961 when he "let every nation know, whether it wishes us well or ill, that we shall pay any price, bear any burden, meet any hardship, support any friend, oppose any foe, to assure the survival and the success of liberty." And it didn't agree with President George W. Bush eight presidents later when he said, "The advance of freedom is the calling of our time; it is the calling of our country...And we believe that freedom—the freedom we prize—is not for us alone, it is the right and capacity of all mankind."

George W. Bush had come to the presidency in the "holiday period" between the Cold War and 9/11, a nine-year interval in which the State Department was realigning itself. They had failed in their four decades of attempting to bring about "peaceful coexistence" between the United States and the Soviet Union. Instead, the Soviet Union was dead. That was not part of their script.

They hoped others would forget their opinions of the past, particularly during the Reagan administration:

"The Evil Empire? Is the White House Cowboy crazy?"
"Now he's done it. That could mean World War III!"
"Did you hear what he just said in West Berlin?"
"I'm afraid to ask."
"'Mr. Gorbachev, tear down this wall!'"
"Find a bomb shelter."

They had been so successful influencing President Carter that they were astounded by their failure in their attempts to influence President Reagan. They then attained some success with President Bush (41) and more success with President Clinton. Now they were faced with the "New Cowboy," President Bush (43).

One of their worst days was Wednesday, April 25, 2001. President George W. Bush had been in office only three months and five days when he appeared on ABC's *Good Morning America.*

"It's premature. Let's hope Charlie Gibson doesn't ask him anything about foreign policy."

But he did.

ABC's Charlie Gibson asked the president: "I'm curious if you, in your own mind, feel that if Taiwan were attacked by China, do we have an obligation to defend the Taiwanese?"

"Yes we do," the president answered. "And the Chinese must understand that. Yes, I would."

"With the full force of the American military?"

"Whatever it took to help Taiwan defend theirself."

His answer created an emotional landslide among the majority of U.S. foreign service officers in the U.S. State Department. (The president obviously meant, "Whatever it would take to help Taiwan defend itself," but it wasn't the syntax, it was the meaning of the words that struck the State Department as being "totally counterproductive.")

"My God, he doesn't know. He just doesn't know."

"He's too new."

"He doesn't know."

"He should have asked us first. We've got to get to Colin Powell and he's got to get to Bush to stop this stuff. He has to retract that statement in some way. He's worse than Reagan. There goes stability."

Foreign service officers had long ago learned that their advancement within the department had a great deal to do with their ability to maintain the department's ever-present belief that stability is the highest imperative of foreign policy.

"Wasn't it Patrick Henry who said 'Give me stability or give me death'?"

"I think so."

"He was a brilliant man."

It took three years and nine months for the State Department to *"free our policy"* from President Bush's April 25, 2001, statement regarding the defense of Taiwan. It was near the end of 2004 and someone had to do something before the imminent changes at the State Department under Condoleezza Rice, which were scheduled to take effect in little more than a month. On December 10, 2004, Deputy Secretary of State Richard L. Armitage appeared with Charlie Rose on the Public Broadcasting System. The deputy secretary was asked, "Where is the landmines—in terms of China's rise and the United States? What has to—."

Deputy Secretary Armitage quickly interrupted to answer, "I would say Taiwan. Taiwan is one. It's probably the biggest."

Charlie Rose asked, "We will defend China from Taiwan if they attack?" (He obviously meant to ask, "We will defend Taiwan from China if they attack?")

This was the opportunity on a silver platter for the deputy secretary of state to finally "correct" President Bush's earlier statement that the United States would do whatever it took to help Taiwan defend itself, although as an officer of the State Department he had to do it with at least some of the instinctive self-preservation that permeated the department through its habitual use of ambiguity.

"Well, I'm, you know, to make a statement like that is not quite appropriate. We have the requirement with the Taiwan Relations Act to keep sufficient force in the Pacific to be able to deter attack. We are not required to defend. And these are questions that actually reside with the U.S. Congress who has to declare an act of war."

"Good man. That took guts. Did you hear that? 'We are not required to defend.'"

"And that it's the Congress that decides, meaning it's not the president's decision. What do you think Bush will say when he learns what Armitage said?"

"Nothing. He knows now not to infuriate China. China will continue to act like they're on our side in the Six Power Talks with North Korea if we keep on our kid gloves. If China's Hu Jintao is lucky, those talks will go on without resolution and drift on and on for a long, long time."

"Do you think Bush remembers he said he'd do whatever it takes to defend Taiwan?"

"It's best that everyone forgets. Besides, that was before 9/11."

It was.

The attacks of September 11, 2001, on the World Trade Center in New York, the Pentagon outside Washington, D.C., and the sky-jacked airliner that was brought down by passengers over Pennsylvania's Somerset County before it could hit another target, were a declaration of war against the United States by Islamist revolutionaries. In one morning 2,973 people were killed in those attacks on United States territory leaving thousands more with physical injuries, the grief of the countless, and other psychological casualties that will never be able to be calculated.

Whatever the president had planned for his administration was reconstituted in the days, weeks, months and years after the morning of 9/11. Defeat in this war would be the end of the United States and, in fact, the end of modern civilization.

One of the many changes was in striving for a status quo to be maintained in all possible armed conflicts other than the war against Islamist terrorism, so that the energy of the United States would be cohesive against the current threat. U.S. armed forces would be spread far enough; thinly spread since the military had been cut to the bone in the 1990s under what had been called the "Peace Dividend."

Under the post-9/11 conditions, conflicts of others could not take precedence over defense of our own nation. Armed conflict anywhere could be a detour whether it would be between Pakistan and India over Kashmir, Greece and Turkey over Cyprus, Turkey and the Kurds, Serbia and Kosovo, the Hutus and Tutsis in Burundi and Rwanda, Northern Ireland and the Republic of Ireland, Spain and the Basques, or the People's Republic of China and Taiwan.

Hu Jintao, president of the People's Republic of China (PRC) knew how to take advantage of the position of the United States. He gave the public impression that he was on the side of the United States in its war against Islamist terrorism while his nation was supplying military supplies and technology to governments supporting Islamist terrorists. His prime card was agreeing to "take the lead" in what became known as the Six-Power Talks (the United States, Japan, Russia, South Korea, North Korea, and China) "to reduce the nuclear threat of North Korea."

The U.S. State Department helped China's President Hu Jintao by challenging statements made by President Chen of Taiwan "as a change in the status quo" even when it came to President Chen's call for democratic referenda of Taiwan's population. Simultaneously the State Department left unchallenged mammoth changes in the status quo committed by China.

Ignored were the severe and direct continued warnings of military action against Taiwan by China, its threats backed up by 400,000 ground forces directly opposite Taiwan with some 700 aircraft and its multiplying deployment of missiles targeted on Taiwan from the Chinese coastline bases across from Taiwan. [They are located in Leping and Ganxian in Jiangxi Province, in Yongan and Xianyou in Fujinan Province, and in Meizhou in Guangdong Province.]

The count of those missiles keeps expanding and the count of today may not be the same as yesterday. According to intelligence estimates, on June 1, 2004, the count was 492 deployed. The count on December 20, 2004, increased to 616 deployed. The count on July 21, 2005, increased to 730 deployed. And the count on January 1, 2006, increased to 784 deployed.

In addition, during the years 2000 through 2005, China had eleven military exercises that simulated an amphibious invasion of Taiwan.

When Porter Goss was director of the Central Intelligence Agency, he testified on February 16, 2005 to the Senate Select Committee on Intelligence that "China continues to develop more robust, survivable nuclear-armed missiles as well as conventional capabilities." Vice Admiral Lowell Jacoby testified to the Senate Armed Services Committee on March 15, 2005, that China was engaged in developing new missile systems [the DF-31, DF-31A, and DF-31S mobile intermediate-range ballistic missiles as well as JL-2 submarine missiles.] China has enlarged, and continues to enlarge, its scope of naval influence deeper into the Pacific, which could potentially threaten oil shipments and physical isolation of its neighbors, including Japan.

Deng Xiaoping had stated, "Hide our capabilities and hide our time; be good at maintaining a low profile, and never claim leadership."

The Defense Intelligence Agency had earlier estimated that China had a total of 157 nuclear warheads that could be used on short-range, medium-range, and Intercontinental Ballistic Missiles (ICBMs) capable of reaching the United States. General Xiong

Guangkai of the People's Republic of China gave a clear warning that the People's Republic of China could launch ICBMs on the United States if the U.S. came to the defense of the people on Taiwan during an attempt of China to take Taiwan. The general asked would the U.S. "sacrifice Los Angeles to protect Taipei?"

That question was part of the most potent weapon system ever devised by man: fear. The weapon of fear injected in individuals and in nations moves with more speed than any other weapon and, throughout history, has most often brought about accommodation, appeasement, and white flags.

Enter President Bush's nomination of Condoleezza Rice as secretary of state in the president's second term to the discouragement of a bureaucracy that largely regarded liberty as a frequent impediment to their objective of hand-shaking and back-slapping and wine-sipping with any current government of the world. The nominee as their secretary, however, believed in President Bush's quest for world liberty.

On Wednesday, January 26, 2005, Condoleezza Rice's nomination was confirmed by the U.S. Senate and she was sworn into office later that day. The following morning she appeared at the U.S. State Department where she received a welcome of applause and cheers from the State Department employees waiting for her in the building's lobby. Of course they gave her applause and cheers. They're diplomats.

Diplomats are not paid to be honest. They are paid to practice diplomacy. To be fair, as we look back at the twentieth century, just think of the wars diplomats prevented. Although none come to mind, there must have been some.

CHAPTER TWO

WHEN IT STARTED

THE GOVERNMENT of the People's Republic of China (PRC) claims possession of Taiwan. It is true that at different periods of history Taiwan has been under the jurisdiction of the emperor of China and the Republic of China (ROC). But it has also been under the jurisdiction of Portugal, the Netherlands, Spain, Japan, and more recently by its own population as a democracy. It has never, not even for a minute, been under the jurisdiction of the *People's* Republic of China. That flag has never been raised over Taiwan. That name has never been adopted in Taiwan. That government has never been accepted in Taiwan. That system has never been established in Taiwan. Yet the government of the People's Republic of China refers to Taiwan as its "renegade province," which it will take by "non-peaceful means" if necessary.

It would make more sense for Great Britain's prime minister to claim the United States of America as a renegade province of the United Kingdom. With even greater logic, Japan's prime minister could make the claim that Taiwan is a renegade province of Japan since Japan was granted possession of Taiwan *in perpetuity* by China in the 1895 Treaty of Shimonoseki. (It was signed by the plenipotentiary Li Hung-chang for the emperor of China.) Japan held Taiwan for fifty years, from 1895 until 1945 when World War II ended and did not *officially* surrender Taiwan until September 8, 1951, when its representatives signed the San Francisco Peace Treaty. Chapter II, Article 2 stated, "Japan renounces all right, title, and claim to Formosa [the Portuguese name for Taiwan] and the Pescadores [islands]." Note that Japan renounced its jurisdiction of Taiwan but did not surrender Taiwan to any particular power.

Without taking too much time and space, this is when it all started:

For millennia, including centuries before the birth of Jesus Christ, China was ruled by emperors of dynasties all the way to October 10, 1911. That was when a rather amazing forty-five-year-old physician named Sun Yat-sen succeeded in leading the revolution that rid China of the Manchu (Qing) Dynasty and, in fact, rid China of all those thousands of years of dynasties. It all became official a few months later on January 1, 1912.

Sun Yat-sen was a great admirer of those things he knew about the United States of America, and particularly about Abraham Lincoln. He advocated what he called the "Three Principles of the People: Nationalism, Democracy, and Social Well-being," creating the first constitutional republic in Asia. In short time he initiated elections of a legislature and created a political party to be known as the Nationalists, better known as the Kuomintang. It won a majority, although the necessary institutions of democracy beyond that election were not built. His plan was to build those institutions in stages—long-evolving stages. There was plenty of opposition to his ideas, opposition to his leadership, and opposition to his Kuomintang Party.

In two years he was overthrown, his Kuomintang was in shambles and he went into exile in Japan. But he came back to China. With the help of the communists—of all things—including the Soviet Union (hardly Lincolnian allies), he won back pockets of territory. He probably felt he needed the communists to gain power and that he could control them, but knowing what he was thinking is theoretical. In 1925 he died, and in death he acquired more power and wider affection than he had in life, which is the test of greatness in world leadership.

The Kuomintang came back after three years of rivalries to take over China. The Kuomintang's leadership was in the hands of Chiang Kai-shek. He did not, however, continue with Sun Yat-sen's plan of an eventual democracy.

Chiang Kai-shek's rule of China lasted through wars with Japan and the communists. The war with Japan stretched into World War II, won by the allies, including Chiang Kai-shek's China.

(The preceding pre-World War II summaries took place before this author's time and therefore are things learned from writings and what was told in later years. I cannot vouch for their accuracy. I also eliminated historical incidents that have little or no effect on current events.)

Among all the events that were brought about by the victory of the allies ending World War II was the establishment of the United Nations, its charter coming into force on October 24, 1945. "The Big Five" allies of World War II were given permanent U.N. Security Council status with veto power. In the order itemized in the U.N. Charter those five nations were: "The Republic of China, France, the Union of Soviet Socialist Republics, the United Kingdom of Great Britain and Northern Ireland, and the United States of America" (Chapter 5, Article 23 of the Charter).

Four years after the United Nations was founded and its Charter was put into effect, Mao Tse-tung's communist revolution overpowered China, defeating the government of the Republic of China led by Chiang Kai-shek. Chiang's leadership of China was over on October 1, 1949, when the victorious Mao Tse-tung raised a new flag over China, changing its name to the *People's* Republic of China and changing its system to communism.

The vanquished government of Chiang Kai-shek, along with over one million followers, sought and attained refuge on Taiwan, which they considered to be part of the Republic of China. From Taiwan, Chiang Kai-shek also claimed that the Republic of China, and not the People's Republic of China, was still the "legal government of the mainland of China" and he pledged that it would someday be recovered by the Kuomintang.

The United States correctly perceived the loss of Chiang's ability to retain his government over China as a catastrophic downfall of a friend and ally in World War II. "Who lost China?" became a campaign issue in the U.S. presidential campaigns of 1952, 1956, and 1960. There was no dispute in the United States among major candidates or political parties that Mao Tse-tung's revolutionary government should not be recognized by the United States as the legal government of China, and that the U.S. recognition of the Republic of China should remain unchanged, as it was ousted by force.

Chiang Kai-shek's Republic of China also retained its seat on the Security Council and in the General Assembly of the United Nations. Most Western countries and many others hoped Chiang Kai-shek would be successful in his advocacy of winning back China on the continent, but few if any believed he had the power or ability.

Shortly after Mao Tse-tung's takeover of China, Mao Tse-tung made his first statement warning that the People's Republic of China would take over Taiwan by force if it did not come into "the embrace of the Motherland" peacefully, and that was when he started using the phrase that continues to be used by the People's Republic of China all the way to today in the consistent statement by the leaders of the People's Republic of China that Taiwan is a "renegade province." (That phrase is similar to the designation given to Kuwait by Iraq's Saddam Hussein as "Iraq's Nineteenth Province" and of Bosnia by Serbia's Slobodan Milosevic as "having been incorporated into the Kingdom of Serbs, Croats, and Slovenes and became one of the six Republics of Yugoslavia.")

Neither Chiang Kai-shek's Kuomintang (KMT) government in Taiwan or Mao Tse-tung's Communist Party (CCP) government in China had any desire to bring about democracies. Chiang Kai-shek's newcomers to Taiwan comprised a 14 percent minority, and to the dissatisfaction of the Taiwanese, who comprised an over-whelming majority of the population, Chiang Kai-shek imposed martial law even before he and most of his Chinese followers ar-rived in Taiwan. According to reports, on February 28, 1947, over two years before he arrived, an elderly Taiwanese woman selling cigarettes without a license was beaten by soldiers of the Kuomin-tang army. There was a demonstration of 2,000 against the Kuomin-tang in Taipei and demonstrations of protest started taking place against the military throughout Taiwan. The officers of the military answered to Governor Chen Yi of Taiwan under the command of Chiang Kai-shek in China, who sent additional troops to Taiwan to quell the protests. Those combined Kuomintang troops ended up killing an estimated 18,000 to 28,000 people. (It took a very unique leader, President Lee Teng-hui of the Kuomintang Party, to publicly apologize in 1995 on behalf of the Kuomintang for what was done some forty-eight years earlier.)

Chiang Kai-shek's imposition of martial law continued with his ar-rival on December 10, 1949, prohibiting opposing political parties to his Kuomintang Party, including the imprisoning of dissidents invok-ing what he called "Temporary Provisions Effective During the Period of Mobilization for the Suppression of the Communist Rebellion."

But the news was even worse for Taiwan from across the Taiwan Strait: Mao Tse-tung's threats to take Taiwan by force did not diminish but increased in frequency and intensity. Neither long-term fate prescribed by "either China" was wanted by the native Taiwanese.

Of the two competing rulers, Chiang Kai-shek's greatest virtue was that he wasn't Mao Tse-tung.

In the late 1950s and throughout the 1960s, the policies of Mao Tse-tung's People's Republic of China, carried out in large part by his premier Chou En-lai, received worldwide attention and horror. There was Mao's "Great Leap Forward" land-reform program that resulted in the death of an estimated 25 million Chinese. This was closely followed by the Cultural Revolution that encouraged the youth to "eliminate" those who existed between Mao and the people, with Mao as the only father of the youth. Adult citizens were ordered to report their thoughts to students twice a day and ordered to perform "loyalty dances" each day in front of their children. Persecution, including the murder of teachers, academics, artists, doctors, and professional people of all fields (including government workers) was encouraged and became commonplace. Millions were killed with the total amount never recorded.

Young people were given *The Little Red Book* of "Quotations from Chairman Mao Tse-tung" to read repeatedly and to wave in demonstrations. Within its pages Mao wrote:

> The enemy will not perish of himself. Neither the Chinese re-actionaries nor the aggressive forces of U.S. imperialism in China will step down from the stage of history of their own accord...Every communist must grasp the truth, that power grows out of the barrel of a gun...Only with guns can the whole world be transformed...First, we must be ruthless to our enemies, we must overpower and annihilate them...It is the Americans themselves who have put nooses round their own necks, handing the ends of the ropes to the Chinese people, the people of Arab countries, and all the peoples of the world who love peace and oppose aggression. The longer the U.S. aggressors remain in those places, the tighter the nooses round their necks will become.

By and large, the communist governments of the world and some third-world governments agreed with Chairman Mao.

CHAPTER THREE

UPHEAVAL IN THE UNITED NATIONS

MAO TSE-TUNG became more and more infuriated with the United Nations retaining the government of Chiang Kai-shek and not permitting membership for his own government, which had taken over China. In response to the U.N., Chairman Mao threatened to join with President Sukarno of Indonesia (who had resigned from the U.N.) in starting an international competition with the U.N. by forming an organization called the "Conference of New Emerging Forces" (CONEFO).

Seventy-seven nations (the majority of U.N. members at the time) were ready to join CONEFO, but the long-delayed first meeting in Indonesia was called off because of a change of government in Indonesia in 1967. The new Indonesian leader who replaced General Sukarno was General Suharto who was an avid anti-communist. He broke diplomatic relations with both the People's Republic of China and the Soviet Union while removing all communists from the Indonesian Parliament. In addition, Suharto re-established diplomatic relations with Western nations and re-enrolled Indonesia into the U.N., rejecting the idea of a competing organization.

But that did not deter Mao. Mao's People's Republic of China vowed to continue organizing the CONEFO as long as the Republic of China (Taiwan) was in the U.N. and the *People's* Republic of China's governance was considered illegal. But CONEFO lost steam and never became a world force as a viable organization.

Those U.N. members who had originally agreed to become members in CONEFO continued to press for the ouster of the Republic of China from the U.N. and for the admission of the People's Republic of China. Each year Mao gained more and more adherents of support in the U.N. and the future acceptance of his government appeared more and more likely.

By the time President Nixon entered the White House in 1969 the avalanche of worldwide support for the People's Republic of China entering the U.N. seemed unstoppable.

Although there was no *public* dialogue between the United States and the People's Republic of China, there was a *private* and secret link for communications through U.S. Ambassador to Poland Walter Stoessel. That link was engaged in planning what became a mid-1971 trip for President Nixon's National Security Council advisor, Henry Kissinger, to go to Peking.

That trip had its public climax on July 15, 1971, when, to the surprise of the world, President Nixon gave the following televised message:

> Good evening. I have requested this television time tonight to announce a major development in our efforts to build a lasting peace in the world. As I have pointed out on a number of occasions over the past three years, there can be no stable peace and enduring peace without the participation of the People's Republic of China and its 750 million people. That is why I have undertaken initiatives in several areas to open the door for more normal relations between our two countries.
>
> In pursuance of that goal, I sent Dr. Kissinger, my assistant for national security affairs, to Peking during his recent world tour for the purpose of having talks with Premier Chou En-lai. The announcement I shall now read is being issued simultaneously in Peking and in the United States:
>
> "Premier Chou En-lai and Dr. Henry Kissinger, President Nixon's assistant for national security affairs, held talks in Peking from July 9 to 11, 1971. Knowing of President Nixon's expressed desire to visit the People's Republic of China, Premier Chou En-lai, on behalf of the government of the People's Republic of China, has extended an invitation to President Nixon to visit China at an appropriate date before May 1972. President Nixon has accepted the invitation with pleasure. The meeting between the leaders of China and the United States is to seek the normalization of relations between the two countries and also to exchange views on questions of concern to the two sides."

In anticipation of the inevitable speculation which will follow this announcement, I want to put our policy in the clearest possible context. Our action in seeking a new relationship with the People's Republic of China will not be at the expense of our old friends. It is not directed against any other nation. We seek friendly relations with all nations. Any nation can be our friend without being any other nation's enemy.

I have taken this action because of my profound conviction that all nations will gain from a reduction of tensions and a better relationship between the United States and the People's Republic of China. It is in this spirit that I will undertake what I deeply hope will become a journey for peace, peace not just for our generation but for future generations on this earth we share together.

Thank you and good night.

On August 4, 1971, Secretary of State William Rogers issued a statement that said in part:

No question of Asian policy has so perplexed the world in the last twenty years as the China question—and the related question of representation in the United Nations. Basic to that question is the fact that each of two governments claims to be the sole government of China and representative of all the people of China...The United States accordingly will support action at the General Assembly this fall calling for seating the People's Republic of China. At the same time the United States will oppose any action to expel the Republic of China or otherwise deprive it representation in the United Nations.

Our consultations which began several months ago have indicated that the question of China's seat in the Security Council is a matter which many nations will wish to address. In the final analysis, of course, under the charter provision, the Security Council will make this decision. We, for our part, are prepared to have this question resolved on the basis of a decision of members of the United Nations. Our consultations have also shown that any action to deprive the Republic of China of its representation would meet strong opposition in the General Assembly. Certainly, as I have said, the United States will oppose it.

The Republic of China has played a loyal and conscientious

role in the U.N. since the organization was founded. It has lived up to all of its charter obligations. Having made remarkable progress in developing its own economy, it has cooperated internationally by providing valuable technical assistance to a number of less-developed countries, particularly in Africa...

Thus, the United States will cooperate with those who, whatever their view on the status of the relationship of the two governments, wish to continue to have the Republic of China represented in the United Nations...

As expected, the Republic of China on Taiwan was strongly opposed to United States support for seating the People's Republic of China in the U.N., but what was unexpected was the statement of the People's Republic of China saying the United States was continuing "to obstruct the restoration to the People's Republic of China of all her legitimate rights in the U.N. and insists on being the enemy of the Chinese people." The People's Republic of China would not take part in any compromise, insisting that as well as potentially achieving a seat of its own in the U.N., the Republic of China on Taiwan had to be expelled from the organization.

On October 18, 1971, four months prior to President Nixon's scheduled trip to Peking, the annual debate in the U.N. began, but positions of most member states were already known. It was apparent that the majority of states would vote for Taiwan to be expelled from the organization. As a result of counting the prospective votes, U.S. Ambassador to the U.N. George Herbert Walker Bush presented a new U.S. position, this one calling for the People's Republic of China to have the Security Council seat while retaining the Republic of China on Taiwan as a member of the U.N. in the General Assembly.

In an evening session of the U.N. on October 25, 1971, twenty-six years after the founding of the U.N. almost to the day, the communist government of Albania submitted a General Assembly Resolution (bypassing the Security Council) mandating the membership of the People's Republic of China into the U.N. and the expulsion of the Republic of China from all organs of the U.N.

The resolution (U.N. General Assembly Resolution 2758) read:

Recalling the principles of the Charter of the United Nations, considering the restoration of the lawful rights of the People's Republic of China is essential both for the protection of the Charter of the United Nations and for the cause that the United Nations must serve under the Charter, recognizing that the representatives of the Government of the People's Republic of China are the only lawful representatives of China to the United Nations and that the People's Republic of China is one of the five permanent members of the Security Council, decides to restore all rights to the People's Republic of China and to recognize the representatives of its Government as the only legitimate representatives of China to the United Nations, and to expel forthwith the representatives of Chiang Kai-shek from the place which they unlawfully occupy at the United Nations and in all the organizations related to it.

The Albanian resolution was, of course, filled with statements that were totally inaccurate at best, known even by those who endorsed the resolution. The most prominent of those weird interpretations of history being "restoration of the lawful rights of the People's Republic of China" when they never had them to restore; "the People's Republic of China is one of the five permanent members of the Security Council" but had never been one of the five permanent members of the Security Council; "expel forthwith the representatives of Chiang Kai-shek from the place which they unlawfully occupy at the United Nations." It was totally within the law of the U.N. and Chiang Kai-shek's representatives occupied its seats in both the Security Council and the General Assembly of the U.N. as one of its founders in 1945 before the People's Republic of China existed.

But, as usual, lies caused nothing but yawns to most fellow diplomats, and it was known that the majority of the members would vote for the Albanian resolution.

Recognizing the votes to come, U.S. Ambassador to the U.N. George Herbert Walker Bush presented a resolution to make the issue an "important question." The phrase "important question" was a procedural designation in the U.N. meaning that an issue would require a *two-thirds* majority for approval rather than requiring a *simple* majority. He was counting on seven members whose representatives told him they would vote for the U.S. resolution.

They didn't. The U.S. resolution lost in a 59–55 vote with 15 abstentions.

That signaled that the end was only minutes away. In view of the obvious, the Republic of China's foreign minister, Chow Shu-kai, and the Republic of China's ambassador to the United Nations, Liu Chieh, led their delegation out of the building. The vote came: of the 131 member-states at the time, the Albanian resolution was passed by 76 to 35 with 17 abstentions, which meant the Republic of China on Taiwan was expelled, and the People's Republic of China was given the Security Council and General Assembly seats the Republic of China had occupied since the founding of the U.N.

There was cheering in the chamber as well as dancing in the aisles of the U.N., the dancing led by Tanzanian ambassador Salim Ahmed Salim.

U.S. ambassador Bush called the vote a "moment of infamy," the first time the word "infamy" was publicly used to describe an international incident by an official of the United States government since President Roosevelt said "...a date which will live in infamy..." to describe the December 7, 1941, attack on Pearl Harbor by the Empire of Japan.

Reactions to the seating of the People's Republic of China and the ejection of the Republic of China came immediately:

President Chiang Kai-shek of Taiwan called the vote an illegal action and called the People's Republic of China "the common enemy of all Chinese people," with the U.N. having "bowed to the forces of evil and violence."

The People's Republic of China issued a statement saying that the U.N. majority expressed "the complete bankruptcy on the policy long pursued by U.S. imperialism in obstructing the restoration of all the lawful rights of our country in the U.N. and of the U.S. scheme of attempting to create two Chinas in the U.N."

U.S. senator from New York James Buckley summed up the reaction of U.S. supporters of Taiwan by saying: "The action taken by the General Assembly may well be recorded as the beginning of the end of the U.N., marking that clear moment when a majority of the member nations decided to abandon principle in order to curry favor with a government which still remains branded by the U.N. as an aggressor: a government which by precept and action repudiates provisions of the U.N. Charter."

Then came 1972 and the promised trip of President Nixon to the People's Republic of China.

It took place in a radically politically changed world from the world of only months earlier: the People's Republic of China now had a distinguished place on the stage of the world's most prestigious international organization, the Republic of China had no seat at all, and the United Nations organization had exhibited its immorality in giving precedence and honor to the forced rule of China by Mao Tse-tung.

CHAPTER FOUR

THE SHANGHAI COMMUNIQUE

PRESIDENT NIXON'S February 1972 trip to China was praised by most governments of the world. There was no praise, of course, from Taiwan, South Vietnam, and South Korea, the three Asian nations most concerned with the increasing international status of their enemy in wars: the People's Republic of China. The Soviet Union publicly praised President Nixon's trip but it was common knowledge that Soviet general secretary Leonid Brezhnev was wary of any handshakes between the United States and the People's Republic of China. The two most prominent communist governments in the world had a history of embracing and then leaving each other at the altar. Mao believed the Soviet Union was best under the late Joseph Stalin, and while under Khrushchev, then Kosygin and Brezhnev, Mao repeatedly complained of "Soviet hegemony [expansionism] and further hegemonistic ambitions." President Nixon's objective was to drive that wedge further between the People's Republic of China and the Soviet Union, reducing the potential of a USSR-PRC alliance. It was, as he called it, "triangulation" between those two powers, using the United States as the third corner of the triangle while retaining U.S. diplomatic relations with the ROC and not giving diplomatic relations to the PRC.

Within the United States there was considerable debate between those who praised President Nixon's trip and those who opposed it. The greatest point of contention was "The Shanghai Communiqué," which was issued the day before President Nixon ended his trip to China. Most of the communiqué dealt with Vietnam and also the Pakistan/India dispute, but, with good reason, the spotlight was on the paragraph that referred to the People's Republic of China and Taiwan.

Prior to the release of the Shanghai Communiqué, President Nixon told China's premier Chou En-lai that the United States did not support the independence movement of Taiwan, (which, at the time, the government of Taiwan itself prohibited to the point of jailing such Taiwanese proponents of independence) but if the call for independence should come about, President Nixon said the United States did not have the authority to prevent it. Chou probably did not believe him. It must be understood that in 1972, at the time of President Nixon's trip, both governments of the People's Republic of China and Taiwan were united in their opposition to the independence of Taiwan, each government for different reasons. (Taiwan's government did not retain that position after democracy was enacted in later years.)

In 1972 Chiang Kai-shek's position was that his Kuomintang was the legal government of China and his party would come back to "the mainland" and take jurisdiction of it as well as retaining Taiwan. Mao's position was also that Taiwan was part of China, but that his People's Republic of China was the legal government of China, including Taiwan.

As President Nixon later recalled (as close as possible to his words): "The words expressed in our Shanghai Communiqué were not about U.S. policy but a statement of different views held by the United States on one side and the People's Republic of China on the other side regarding a number of issues—not of agreements between our two sides, but statements of our side's position and statements of their side's position and they were labeled in the communiqué as such—as exactly that." He went on to read the communiqué. (Italics are used here for words he accented as he reread the communiqué. Words in parentheses were not in the communiqué but his words, or close to them, in explanation of the communiqué.)

> The part of the communiqué pertaining to Taiwan was "The U.S. side declared: the United States *acknowledges* (not our policy but an acknowledgment of the truth as it existed then) that all *Chinese* (meaning those Chinese who came to Taiwan, and the Chinese represented by the People's Republic of China—not the native Taiwanese or we would have used the

word "people" instead of "Chinese") on either side of the Taiwan Strait maintain there is but one China and that Taiwan is a part of China. (That was correct in 1972. The dispute back then was over which of the two governments would have jurisdiction of both entities.) The United States government does not challenge that position. (Why should we when both sides agreed?) With this prospect in mind, it affirms the *ultimate* objective of the withdrawal of all U.S. forces and military installations from Taiwan. (It's always been our policy and serves our national interest that when a friend gets out of jeopardy, we leave.) In the meantime, it will progressively reduce its forces and military installations on Taiwan *as the tension in the area diminishes*. (It has to diminish for this to take effect.) The two sides agreed that it is desirable to broaden the understanding between the two peoples. To this end, they discussed specific areas in such fields as science, technology, culture, sports, and journalism in which people-to-people (as you know, that's Ike's old phrase he initiated in 1956 in international contacts: people-to-people) contacts and exchanges would be mutually beneficial. Each side undertakes to facilitate the further development of such contacts and exchanges." (You will notice that I did not make a statement regarding who governed China, the PRC or the ROC, which was the issue of the time.)

That communiqué became intentionally misinterpreted by the U.S. State Department and that intentional misinterpretation became the foundation of two future communiqués, one to come in the Carter administration and the other in the Reagan administration. Out of that intentional misinterpretation that became more pronounced as the years went on, the United States government adopted the position that the People's Republic of China is the legal government of China and Taiwan is part of the People's Republic of China, a statement that had never been made in the U.S. position as given or intended or anticipated or written in the Shanghai Communiqué.

It could be argued that the error of the communiqué was in stating only the positions of the Chinese on either side of the Taiwan Strait and not giving the position of the native Taiwanese or any of those who were in Taiwan as descendents of Chinese before Chiang Kai-shek came to Taiwan in 1949. However, most throughout the world viewed the dispute as one between a communist government (Mao's) and an anti-communist government (Chiang's) and that dispute was paramount. Since, in those days, most of the countries of the world were non-democracies, the fact that Chiang did not rule by democratic institutions was not the prime concern. The Cold War dictated that the prime concern of governments (democratic and non-democratic) had to be the victories or defeats of communist countries.

Because the alternative to Chiang Kai-shek would be Mao Tse-tung, there was no contest in terms of our support for Chiang. Most of those Americans who today believe in Taiwan's independence and most of those Americans who today are opposed to its independence were supporters of Chiang Kai-shek back in those days. If the native Taiwanese had an active political establishment back then, there would then have been an internationally known third force. But there was no bona fide political body for independence, as Chiang Kai-shek and his Kuomintang political party prevented those Taiwanese for independence from organizing into a political party or any feasible world-known entity.

The flood of events regarding Taiwan and China was not done. When political events rested, events of nature took over. In a period of only seventeen months the leaders of both Taiwan and China died. Chiang Kai-shek of the Republic of China on Taiwan died in April 1975, and was replaced by his son, Chiang Ching-kuo. The People's Republic of China's premier, Chou En-lai, died in January 1976, and was replaced by Hua Kuo-feng (and later replaced by Zhao Ziyang, then Li Peng, then Zhu Rongji, then Wen Jiabo). Mao Tse-tung died eight months after Chou En-lai in September 1976, followed by a power struggle.

That power struggle would not be won until 1978 by Teng Hsiao-ping (Deng Xiaoping) who would later become known as "The Paramount Leader" of the People's Republic of China. Not even Mao had that prestigious title. Knowing Mao's history, it probably wasn't humility, but because he never thought of it. If he is somewhere where he can look at the world today, it's likely that he's upset he settled for "Chairman." At this date, he will just have to accept it.

CHAPTER FIVE

A SURPRISE UNDER THE CHRISTMAS TREE

THERE WERE very few political residents still in Washington, D.C., ten days before Christmas in 1978. Most members of the congress had already gone back home; it was difficult to reach leading bureaucrats in their offices as they were out shopping; little by little appointees were packing to get out of D.C. until a scheduled return just before Tuesday, January 2nd of the new year; and even the media had given up looking for good political stories in this season.

During that early morning of Friday, December 15th, the telephone rang at the residence of former president Richard Nixon at what had been called the Western White House in San Clemente, California (called La Casa Pacifica by the former president). This is as close to word-for-word as can be done:

"Mr. President, you've been told, I'm sure, that President Carter is going to give a speech tonight."

"Tonight?"

"Yes. Prime time. Eight o'clock tonight. If you're considering giving a statement—"

The president interrupted. "What's it about?"

There was some hesitancy. The president's friend had hoped the president had heard about the event to come as he didn't want to be the one to deliver the news, but it was better than leaving the president in the dark. He said it softly: "Mr. President, he's going to give diplomatic recognition to the People's Republic of China."

There was a long pause.

The pause was so long that the friend of the president felt he had to say something to interrupt the silence. "That means, of course, that he's breaking diplomatic relations with Taiwan. The PRC wouldn't allow otherwise, would it?"

After an additional silence the former president responded. "No. No. How good is your source?"

"He's as solid as can be. He's a good man; totally trustworthy. If he's wrong it would be by error, not by intent. And this doesn't sound like error because he just came from a policy meeting about the China initiative that he said President Carter will announce tonight."

"Is it out? Leaked?"

"Not to my knowledge."

"It isn't out? The media didn't get wind of this?"

"I don't know for sure, but I think not. I was told President Carter is going to meet with a congressional delegation in the Roosevelt Room at around 6:30 tonight. Not until then. I was told that later on he's going to meet with some of the media just minutes before giving his speech. I think he's going to meet with them downstairs in the Staff Mess. At least that's the plan right now, as it was told to me."

"Did he tell Taiwan? President Chiang?"

"I don't know. I can't imagine that he didn't."

Again there was a long pause followed by President Nixon saying, "You know, this means not only cutting off recognition of Taiwan, it means abrogating the Mutual Defense Treaty with them that we've had since—since I was VP. John Foster Dulles signed it for Ike in '54. And it means all U.S. troops have to leave Taiwan. That's what they told me we had to do when I went to Peking in '72. They insisted on those three things. That's what they said I had to do if I wanted diplomatic relations. No way! And Jerry [President Gerald Ford] was told the same thing after he became president when he went to China in '75. No way from him, too."

"President Carter didn't tell you anything about this decision of his, Mr. President? At least tell you—if he wasn't going to ask your advice?"

"No." There was a pause and then a question. "You're absolutely sure?"

"In this case I wish I wasn't." There was the silence again. Then, "So do I."

A SURPRISE UNDER THE CHRISTMAS TREE

It was twelve minutes after eight p.m. when President Carter walked into the brightly lit Oval Office, said hello to the television technicians, sat behind his desk, and after a few adjustments began the television transmission. (The most pertinent parts of his speech are printed below.)

Good evening. I would like to read a joint communiqué which is being simultaneously issued in Peking at this very moment by the leaders of the People's Republic of China:

"A Joint Communiqué on the Establishment of Diplomatic Relations Between the United States of America and the People's Republic of China, January 1, 1979.

"The United States of America and the People's Republic of China have agreed to recognize each other and to establish diplomatic relations as of January 1, 1979.

"The United States recognizes the government of the People's Republic of China as the sole legal government of China.

"Within this context the people of the United States will maintain cultural, commercial, and other unofficial relations with the people of Taiwan.

"The United States of America and the People's Republic of China reaffirm the principles agreed on by the two sides in the Shanghai Communiqué of 1972 and emphasize once again that both sides wish to reduce the danger of international military conflict. Neither should seek hegemony—that is, the dominance of one nation over the others—in the Asia-Pacific region or in any other region of the world and each is opposed to efforts by any other country or group of countries to establish such hegemony.

"Neither is prepared to negotiate on behalf of any other third party or to enter into agreements or understandings with the other directed at other states.

"The government of the United States of America acknowledges the Chinese position that there is but one China and Taiwan is part of China.

"Both believe that normalization of Sino-American relations is not only in the interest of the Chinese and American people but also contributes to the cause of peace in Asia and in the world.

"The United States of America and the People's Republic of China will exchange ambassadors and establish embassies on March 1, 1979."

His reading of the communiqué was done and the president looked directly at the television audience.

Yesterday our country and the People's Republic of China reached this final historic agreement. On January 1, 1979, a little more than two weeks from now, our two governments will implement full normalization of diplomatic relations...

These more positive relations with China can beneficially affect the world in which we live and the world in which our children will live.

We have already begun to inform our allies and other nations and the members of the Congress of the details of our intended action, but I wish also tonight to convey a special message to the people of Taiwan.

I have already communicated with the leaders in Taiwan, with whom the American people have had, and will have, extensive, close, and friendly relations. This is important between our two peoples. As the United States asserted in the Shanghai Communiqué of 1972 issued on President Nixon's historic visit, we will continue to have an interest in the peaceful resolution of the Taiwan issue.

I have paid special attention to insuring that normalization of relations between our country and the People's Republic will not jeopardize the well-being of the people of Taiwan.

The people of our country will maintain our current commercial, cultural, trade, and other relations with Taiwan through nongovernmental means. Many other countries of the world are already successfully doing this.

These decisions and these actions open a new and important chapter in our country's history and also in world affairs. To strengthen and to expedite the benefits of this new relationship between China and the United States, I am pleased to announce that Vice Premier Teng Hsiao-ping [Deng Xiaoping] has accepted my invitation and will visit Washington at the end of January. His visit will give our governments the opportunity to consult with each other on global issues and to begin working together to enhance the cause of world peace.

These events are the final result of long and serious negotiations begun by President Nixon in 1972 and continued under the leadership of President Ford. The results bear witness to the steady, determined, bipartisan effort of our own country to build a world in which peace will be the goal and the responsibility of all nations.

The normalization of relations between the United States and China has no other purpose than the advancement of peace. It is in this spirit, at this season of peace, that I take special pride in sharing this good news with you tonight.

Thank you very much.

The television transmission ended. President Carter leaned back in his chair and with comfort he said to no one in particular, "Applause throughout the nation!"

Maybe not throughout the nation, but there was applause throughout the State Department.

Most noticeable in President Carter's communiqué was the way in which the Shanghai Communiqué of President Nixon was misused as the basis for his own communiqué: the Carter Communiqué read, "The United States of America and the People's Republic of China affirm the *principles agreed on* by the two sides in the Shanghai Communiqué." The Shanghai Communiqué was clear in *not* stating "principles" nor was there a statement within the Shanghai Communiqué of the United States and the PRC *agreement* on this issue. Worst of all were the assertions in President Carter's statement that "The United States *recognizes the government of the People's Republic of China* as the *sole legal government* of China…The government of the United States of America acknowledges the Chinese position that there is but one China and *Taiwan is part of China.*"

Those two sentences of the communiqué separated by other statements indicated that, as president, he perceived Taiwan as part of the *People's* Republic of China, radically changing U.S. policy. He used a paraphrase of the "acknowledgment statement" of the

Shanghai Communiqué but preceded it earlier in his speech by recognizing the People's Republic of China as the sole legal government of China. (Years after the Carter Communiqué, the third Joint Communiqué, agreed upon on August 17, 1982, during the Reagan administration, repeated the Carter Communiqué by recording: "In the Joint Communiqué on the Establishment of Diplomatic Relations on January 1, 1979, issued by the Government of the United States of America and the People's Republic of China, the United States of America recognized the Government of the People's Republic of China as the sole legal Government of China, and it acknowledged the Chinese position that there is but one China and Taiwan is part of China....")

Once President Carter's speech was over, there were demonstrations outside the U.S. Embassy in Taipei, Taiwan, protesting President Carter's decision. Taiwan's President Chiang Ching-kuo said: "Now that it has broken the assurances and abrogated the [Mutual Defense] Treaty, the United States government cannot be expected to have the confidence of any free nation in the future." He said the initiative of President Carter was "an unwise and horrible move" and that the United States had "never severed its relations with a friendly country. Now it has done that."

Senator Barry Goldwater threatened that he would take President Carter's decision to abrogate the Mutual Defense Treaty of 1954 to court "and show the action to be both illegal and unconstitutional."

George Meany, the president of the AFL-CIO, said he could not understand "how this president, who made human rights a world issue, could so suddenly and callously reject the human rights concerns of both those enslaved on Mainland China and those on Taiwan who fear such enslavement."

Within twenty-four hours *after* the speech was done, the Carter White House sent a briefing to former president Nixon.

President Nixon maintained the tradition of former U.S. presidents not to publicly criticize a current president. Privately, he was not supportive. Five days after President Carter's speech he sent a personal letter to President Carter, not seen by press or public.

Within his letter he attempted to cloak his anger with understanding, respect for the office held by President Carter, lines of pragmatic politics, some psychology, and most of all, courtesy. But his anger was not successfully masked. The letter follows in its entirety.

December 20, 1978

Dear Mr. President,

After receiving the briefing you thoughtfully provided, I should like to pass on to you my personal views with regard to your decision to normalize relations with the PRC.

I have made no public statement because since your action has already been taken it is now U.S. policy, and I see no constructive purpose to be served by publicly second guessing what you have done. However, I have some views about implementing the policy and on issues relating to it which I think might be useful for you to consider.

First, as to the process by which the agreement was reached, I know from experience that particularly when negotiating with the Chinese, secrecy is indispensable if there is to be any chance for success. The Congress, of course, will have an opportunity to play a role in approving appropriations and other legislation necessary to implement the agreement.

I have three major concerns: the adequacy of the guarantees against the use of force to resolve the Taiwan issue; the credibility of U.S. commitments to our other allies and friends in view of our termination of the Taiwan Treaty; the effect on your ability as President to enlist public support for your other foreign policy initiatives in the future.

No reasonable person would question Dr. Brzezinski's assertion that the PRC, because of its control over population and territory, is in fact the government of China. However, no political realist can ignore the fact that the 17 million people on Taiwan, who have prospered greatly under a non-communist government, have an almost fanatical core of support in the nation and in the Congress. You addressed this problem in your December 15 announcement. I believe, however, that it is essential that you and your representatives give additional reassurances firmly and unequivocally.

I recognize that realistically the possibility of a PRC military attack on Taiwan will be remote for several years. But I believe the U.S. should publicly go on record that any use of force against Taiwan would irreparably jeopardize our relations with the PRC. I believe, also, that we should make it clear that we not only have the right to approve private arms sales to Taiwan, but that we intend to exercise that right for as long and to the degree necessary to deter any use of force against Taiwan. If because of the delicate state of our negotiations with the PRC you feel the administration could not go this far, I would not discourage the Congress from doing so. If the Congress does proceed in that manner I would urge you not to oppose such action publicly and that you privately inform the Chinese of the problem. They will strenuously object, but they will understand because they need us far more than we need them. They also will be impressed by the fact that those who are most strongly pro-Taiwan are also those who are most strongly anti-Soviet.

There are those who contend that the pro-Taiwan forces are stupid, short-sighted, and reckless. Assuming for the sake of argument this to be true, they are a fact of American political life and they are effective. Unless their opposition is mitigated, you will probably still win the battle; but you may lose the war because the fallout on future foreign and defense policy battles you will have to fight will make the Panama Canal controversy look like a Sunday school picnic in comparison.

With regard to the effect of your decision on other allies and friends, I believe it is essential for you to reiterate that Taiwan was a special case and that the U.S. firmly stands by all its treaty and other commitments and under no circumstances will we renounce a treaty simply because we determine our interests are no longer served by it. As a respectful suggestion you might indicate that while you do not give an inch on the proposition that a President has a Constitutional right to rescind a treaty without obtaining Senate approval, you will in the future voluntarily submit such decisions to the Senate.

With regard to specific countries, I am most concerned about Korea. I realize that you have announced a decision to withdraw American forces by 1983. I would strongly urge you to reconsider that decision in view of Soviet supported adventurist policies in Afghanistan, Ethiopia, and other countries in Africa. If you believe you should not do so, I would suggest that at this time it would be most helpful to increase substantially the budget for military aid to Korea as a symbolic move to put North Korea and others on notice that the action on Taiwan should under no circumstances be interpreted as the beginning of a U.S. withdrawal from other parts of Asia.

The Philippines, Indonesia, and Iran in different ways present diffi-

cult problems because of their corruption and in varying degrees their denial of human rights. At this time in view of the Taiwan decision, I believe it is important to publicly and privately give them unqualified support. It would be ironical to qualify our support to any country which allows some human rights at a time when we have dramatically moved toward normalization with full cooperation with a nation which allows none—the PRC.

I don't mean to criticize your eloquent commitment to this cause, but I feel the greatest threat to human rights today is on the totalitarian left rather than on the authoritarian right.

With regard to my third concern, as one who initiated détente with the USSR, I must in all candor say that based on what I have read in the press, I have some grave questions about the terms that are being considered for SALT II. However, I believe it would be most unfortunate if Senators voted against SALT primarily because of resentment on the PRC normalization decision. We hear that some want to "get well" after supporting the Panama treaty. They will not be able to do so on normalization because it is a fait accompli. *They might well take out their frustration on SALT specifically and détente generally. Since a yes vote on Panama has been interpreted as being "soft" they are looking for some way to correct the balance and a no vote on SALT provides that opportunity.*

I believe that this is one of those critical times when you cannot afford any moves which justifiably or not are considered soft or weak, vis-à-vis the Communist powers. For example, any plans even to consider normalization with Cuba or Vietnam should be put on the back burner, which I assume would be your intention anyway in view of their barbaric behavior toward their own people and toward others.

I apologize for the length of this letter and I imagine that many of my suggestions will be like carrying coals to Newcastle, or bringing saki to Nada, as the Japanese would say.

From a purely partisan political standpoint, I would hope you would not take my advice. But I feel that the stakes for America and the world are too high for partisanship as usual. You have a supreme opportunity to lead the nation and the world into a new era of prosperity, peace, and justice. To paraphrase Charlie Wilson— what is good for you is good for America, and if it results in many happy returns for you in 1980, you will deserve it.

Please do not take time to reply to this letter. I have not written it "for the record" and do not intend to make it public. I know that par-

ticularly at this time you are overburdened with work with the final budget decisions to be made, the State of the Union address to be prepared, and a possible Summit visit with Brezhnev on the agenda.

With warm personal regards,

Sincerely,

Richard Nixon

The response from President Carter read in its entirety:

12-22-78

To Pres Richard Nixon

I appreciate your excellent letter, which is very helpful to me. We have, with some difficulty, reserved the options you described in our negotiations with the PRC.

After you receive a final briefing on SALT II, your analysis would also be welcome. This has been a long and laborious process which has a good prospect of coming out well.

Our best wishes to you and your family - Jimmy Carter

What had been the embassy and consulates of the Republic of China on Taiwan were taken over by the People's Republic of China while Taiwan would occupy what would be called the "Coordination Council for North American Affairs" (CCNAA), later to be changed to "Taipei Economic and Cultural Representative Offices" (TECRO). In Taipei our U.S. Embassy was not to be an embassy at all but "The American Institute in Taiwan" (AIT) staffed by retired U.S. foreign service officers. The American Institute's domestic headquarters would be located across the Potomac from Washington, D.C., in Arlington, Virginia, rather than inside the District, to be staffed only by foreign service officers on leave. Even the International Telecommunication Union made Taiwan's telephone country code into the unofficial number of 886, simply labeled as "reserved." The People's Republic of China would not use the code because it was an international one, and was allowed to call Taiwan by dialing 06, which was domestic.

On April 10, 1979, an angry majority of the 96th United States Congress passed the Taiwan Relations Act. It stated that:

> The President, having terminated governmental relations between the United States and the governing authorities on Taiwan recognized by the United States as the Republic of China prior to January 1, 1979, the Congress finds that the enactment of this Act is necessary to help maintain peace, security, and stability in the Western Pacific; and to promote the foreign policy of the United States by authorizing the continuation of commercial, cultural, and other relations between the people of the United States and the people on Taiwan...

> The United States will make available to Taiwan such defense articles and defense services in such quantity as may be necessary to enable Taiwan to maintain a sufficient self-defense capability. The President and the Congress shall determine the nature and quantity of such defense articles and services based solely upon their judgment of the needs of Taiwan, in accordance with procedures established by law. Such determination of Taiwan's defense needs shall include review by United States military authorities in connection with recommendations to the President and the Congress.

> The President is directed to inform the Congress promptly of any threat to the security or the social or economic system of the people on Taiwan and any danger to the interests of the United States arising therefrom. The President and the Congress shall determine, in accordance with constitutional processes, appropriate action by the United States in response to any such danger.

It is the Taiwan Relations Act that has been the key instrument of U.S. policy toward Taiwan since 1979.

Senator Barry Goldwater went through with his earlier threat to bring the abrogation of the Mutual [between the United States and Taiwan] Defense Treaty of 1954 to court. He was joined by twenty-four other members of the Congress. His position was that since two-thirds of the Senate must give advice and consent in concurrence to put a treaty *into* force, the same procedure must be used to *terminate* a treaty. Since the treaty was not to be broken until January 1, 1980, there was still time to prevent the abrogation. (The diplomatic relations decision had already taken effect as of January 1, 1979.)

The U.S. District Court first dismissed the suit on June 6, stating the differences between the executive branch and the legislature should be resolved by those two branches of government. However, it was added that if the Senate or the Congress as a whole took action, "the controversy will be ripe for a judicial declaration."

Within hours the Senate did take action, voting 59 to 35 in a Sense of the Senate Resolution (non-binding) that the U.S. Senate must approve the termination of any "Mutual Defense Treaty between the United States and another nation."

Three more 1979 chapters of the courts followed before it was decided:

October 17: With the Senate making its opinion known, the U.S. District Court reappraised its earlier decision and determined President Carter needed the consent of the Congress to end the Mutual Defense Treaty. Judge Gasch ordered a prohibition of completing the abrogation: "At least under the circumstances of this case, involving a mutual defense treaty with a faithful ally who has not violated the terms of the agreement, and the validity of which has not otherwise been destroyed, any decision of the United States to terminate that treaty must be made with the advice and consent of the Senate or the approval of both Houses of the Congress. This decision cannot be made by the President alone."

November 30: The U.S. Court of Appeals for the District of Columbia ruled by a 4 to 1 vote that President Carter did have the authority to unilaterally terminate the Mutual Defense Treaty of 1954. "The subtleties involved in maintaining amorphous relationships are often the very stuff of diplomacy, a field in which the President, not Congress, has responsibility under our Constitution." [This was a reference to the majority opinion of the U.S. Supreme Court in 1936, written by Justice George Sutherland in *U.S. v. Curtiss-Wright Export Corp.*]

Senator Goldwater then brought the case to the U.S. Supreme Court.

December 13: The U.S. Supreme Court by a vote of 7 to 2 refused to hear the case, its refusal allowing the decision of the U.S. Court of Appeals for the District of Columbia to stand. Since four U.S. Supreme Court Justices are needed to hear a case, the abrogation of the treaty would take effect.

Within the People's Republic of China, Deng Xiaoping was beginning to be perceived as almost a godlike figure. For most of those in the United States it was difficult to share that kind of admiration: he was vice premier of the People's Republic of China in 1952 while the Korean War was being waged with the PRC aiding (and even saving) North Korea. In that war, 36,916 Americans were killed and 103,284 Americans were wounded. He was the vice premier again in 1973 when North Vietnam, with the support and help of the People's Republic of China, violated the Paris Peace Accords. In the Vietnam War, 58,193 Americans were killed and 153,363 Americans were wounded. Deng supported and gave aid to the Khmer Rouge's Pol Pot all the way through and beyond the genocide of Cambodia. In 1978 he ordered the crackdown upon and imprisonment of those who put messages on Beijing's Democracy Wall.

The grandest gift Deng Xiaoping received was in the Christmas season of 1978 when President Carter traded away diplomatic relations between the United States and Taiwan for diplomatic relations between the United States and the People's Republic of China. President Carter had said that evening, "These more positive relations with China can beneficially affect the world in which we live and the world in which our children will live."

He was wrong. Ten and a half years later, in 1989, Deng Xiaoping and Premier Li Peng would order the Tiananmen Square Massacre of thousands of demonstrators wanting, at least, a dialogue with the leadership, and at most, a system of democracy. Deng Xiaoping continued to justify the massacre throughout the rest of his life.

And so did President Carter continue to justify his own decision regarding the Christmas gift of 1978.

CHAPTER SIX

ENDORSEMENTS

IN 1980 Ronald Reagan was elected president of the United States, followed in 1988 by the election of George Herbert Walker Bush. During those administrations, surprisingly there were no meaningful changes in U.S. policy toward Taiwan and China from the agreements made by President Carter. That was a severe disappointment to supporters of Taiwan since, with few exceptions, President Reagan's most ardent followers were also Taiwan's most ardent advocates. Moreover, President Reagan had an iron fist when it came to foreign policy and had a strong history of support for Taiwan. His vice president and a future president of the United States, George Herbert Walker Bush, also had a strong history as the U.S. representative to the United Nations who fought for Taiwan's seat in the U.N.'s General Assembly. (He was later appointed by President Ford to be the first Chief United States Liaison Officer in Peking, which might have influenced his later more amicable feelings toward the PRC.)

As disappointing as it was to so many that President Carter's policies were retained, the reasoning of President Reagan was not only based on the advice of the State Department but was steeped in an important U.S. tradition (and a similar tradition of most democracies) that dictates a new president does not act to void international agreements of previous presidents other than in the most extraordinary circumstances or extreme changing conditions. This tradition was meant to retain consistency in foreign policy and allow foreign nations to regard U.S. agreements as the nation's word rather than an individual president's word. What made the Carter decisions regarding Taiwan and the People's Republic of China so explosive was that they were not in keeping with that tradition.

While democracies generally keep international agreements made by their nation's preceding governments, *non*-democracies generally keep international agreements of their previous governments *only* if they meet the policies of their current government. China is a perfect illustration.

A previous government of China (the emperor of China) signed an agreement with Great Britain (the British Empire) that Hong Kong Island would be Great Britain's property in perpetuity. The People's Republic of China disregarded that international agreement. A previous government of China (the emperor of China) signed an agreement with Great Britain (the British Empire) that the Kowloon peninsula would be Great Britain's property in perpetuity. The People's Republic of China disregarded that international agreement. A previous government of China (the emperor of China) signed an agreement with Japan (the emperor of Japan) that Taiwan would be Japan's property in perpetuity. The People's Republic of China disregarded that international agreement. But when it came to the long-ago possession of Taiwan by the emperor of China, the People's Republic of China insists that the international agreement of a long-ago Chinese emperor be maintained by the now free people of Taiwan. The national inconsistency reached international acceptance by confirming the belief that the word of a previous government of China must be maintained by Taiwan, but not be maintained by China.

Although there were no important *changes* in Taiwan policy in the Reagan and Bush administrations, there were meaningful events that *confirmed* Carter policy in both of those administrations.

On August 17, 1982, President Reagan issued a (State Department authored) communiqué, which became the third communiqué when added to the Shanghai Communiqué of President Nixon and the Communiqué on the Establishment of Diplomatic Relations Between the United States of America and the People's Republic of China of President Carter. President Reagan's communiqué was largely based on President Carter's communiqué. In addition to the previously mentioned part of the Reagan Communiqué, it also read in part:

> Respect for each other's sovereignty and territorial integrity
> and non-interference in each other's internal affairs consti-
> tute the fundamental principles guiding United States–China

relations. These principles were confirmed in the Shanghai Communiqué of February 28, 1972, and reaffirmed in the Joint Communiqué on the Establishment of Diplomatic Relations, which came into effect on January 1, 1979. Both sides emphatically state these principles continue to govern all aspects of their relations.

The United States attaches a great importance to its relations with China, and reiterates that it has no intention of infringing on Chinese sovereignty and territorial integrity, or interfering in China's internal affairs, or pursuing a policy of "two Chinas" or "one China, one Taiwan." [The misinterpretation of the Shanghai Communiqué was similar to the use of it in the Carter Communiqué.]

One month before President Reagan's Communiqué was issued and while discussions with the PRC were in progress, President Reagan sought to clarify U.S. policy to President Chiang Ching-kuo of Taiwan. (The attempted clarification was given without the enthusiasm of the State Department.) President Reagan's statement quickly became known in Taiwan as "The Six Assurances":

1. The United States would not set a date for termination of arms sales to Taiwan.

2. The United States would not alter the terms of the Taiwan Relations Act.

3. The United States would not consult with China in advance before making decisions about U.S. arms sales to Taiwan.

4. The United States would not mediate between Taiwan and China.

5. The United States would not alter its position about the sovereignty of Taiwan, which was that the question was one to be decided peacefully by the Chinese themselves, and would not pressure Taiwan into negotiations with China. [Note the continuing use of the word "Chinese" in this context rather than the words, "Chinese and Taiwanese."]

6. The United States would not formally recognize Chinese sovereignty over Taiwan.

The Six Assurances were greeted with some relief by the people of Taiwan and especially by President Chiang Ching-kuo, who was ending the dictated restrictions placed on the people of Taiwan by his father's administration.

In the U.S. Department of Defense, a contingency plan called Opian 0577 was born regarding options on U.S. actions should the People's Republic of China attack Taiwan. In brief, "all options" were available and "on the table."

By 1987, Chiang Ching-kuo went on to end martial law and lift what had been called the Emergency Decrees of 1949. This new freedom increased the numbers and stature of dissident groups. Large numbers of dissidents had already formed a coalition into a political party: the Democratic Progressive Party (DPP). Chiang Ching-kuo did not enforce its illegality previously proclaimed, and there was no effort to suppress the DPP or other parties that were opposed to the Kuomintang.

President Chiang Ching-kuo died in 1988, and Lee Teng-hui, the vice president who was a native Taiwanese (born during Japan's rule of Taiwan), succeeded Chiang, becoming Taiwan's first home-born president. President Lee brought about the total legalization of opposition political parties in 1989. (One of those parties, the previously mentioned Democratic Progressive Party, would later become the winning party in the 2000 and 2004 presidential elections.)

Other than the Third Communiqué and the Six Assurances, there was one item left on the table of endorsement or non-endorsement following President Carter's presidency: Most Favored Nation (MFN) trade status for the People's Republic of China. (MFN with China had been suspended under President Truman on September 1, 1951, effective July 14, 1952, and restored twenty-seven years later under President Carter's recommendation of July 17, 1979, with approval of the 96th Congress on January 24, 1980.)

Both President Reagan and his successor, President Bush, endorsed its continuation.

An event of tremendous worldwide significance occurred during the Bush (41) administration in June 1989 when demonstrators in the People's Republic of China became the victims of the Tiananmen Square Massacre in which thousands were murdered under the direction and orders of Deng Xiaoping and Premier Li Peng. This was surely one of those extreme changing conditions and extraordinary circumstances that could justifiably cause a U.S. president to change policy directions from prior commitments.

During the demonstration that preceded the massacre, Secretary of State James Baker and National Security Advisor Brent Scowcroft called for "restraint on both sides." The impartiality of that statement needed no translation. It meant our government did not want the PRC's government to kill anyone, but the demonstrators should go home. In short, words of impartiality the PRC welcomed.

After the massacre, President Bush announced sanctions against China with a suspension of military equipment, a suspension of government-to-government trade, an extension of visas for Chinese students already in the United States, and a suspension of any high-level meetings between officials of the United States and the People's Republic of China. But without telling the nation, Deputy Secretary of State Lawrence Eagleburger and National Security Advisor Brent Scowcroft were sent to Beijing in July 1989 within weeks of the massacre. And there were indeed high-level meetings. There was a second secret trip of Deputy Secretary of State Lawrence Eagleburger and National Security Advisor Brent Scowcroft in December of 1989. It must be understood that travels this sensitive are decided on a presidential level, and there is reason to believe that Lawrence Eagleburger was not enthused about or even endorsed the trips to China to which he had been assigned.

A dozen days after the massacre, China's paramount leader, Deng Xiaoping, predicted, "Once the political situation has stabilized and the economy is fueled, the foreigners are going to be back knocking on our door."

Deng was much too pessimistic. The foreigners were back knocking on his door long before he predicted.

CHAPTER SEVEN

IT'S ONLY BUSINESS

ON MARCH 9, 1992, candidate for the U.S. presidency Bill Clinton said, "I do not believe we should extend Most Favored Nation status to China unless they make significant progress in human rights, arms proliferation, and fair trade."

On May 1, 1991, President Lee of Taiwan announced the total abolition of *all* authoritarian and undemocratic laws that had been put in place by Chiang Kai-shek, including the "Temporary Provisions Effective During the Period of Mobilization for the Suppression of the Communist Rebellion," which had given dictatorial powers to the President of Taiwan. In addition, President Lee officially ended the advocacy of the Kuomintang government's 1949 pledge to rule China. That step confirmed that Taiwan was not a threat to the People's Republic of China either in fact or now in words. That was when the term "Taiwan" started to be used more often in that island nation, rather than Chiang Kai-shek's Kuomintang term "the Republic of China." The People's Republic of China was not in any sense relieved to have Taiwan give up its threats as some might have thought. Instead, Deng Xiaoping's government in Beijing preferred the old advocacy of the Republic of China on Taiwan claiming jurisdiction of China rather than have it regard itself as a separate entity. At least when Taiwan threatened to take over China, it regarded itself as *part* of China. In retaliation, the People's Republic of China did not reduce its threats against Taiwan but increased them, accusing it of a "separatist" government.

On October 1, 1992, candidate Clinton said, "There is no more striking example of Mr. Bush's indifference toward democracy than his policy toward China…I do believe that our nation has a higher purpose than to coddle dictators."

On November 3, 1992, candidate Clinton was elected president of the United States, and he was inaugurated on January 20, 1993.

On May 28, 1993, President Clinton, in contrast to his campaign statements, signed an executive order continuing Most Favored Nation (MFN) trade status with China for another year, saying, "We are hopeful that China's process of development and economic reform will be accompanied by greater political freedom. The question we face today is how best to cultivate these hopeful seeds of change in China while expressing our clear disapproval of its repressive policies." He simultaneously mandated that renewal of MFN the following year would be conditional, based on overall significant progress of human rights in China.

The 103rd Congress approved MFN status being continued. (A 1974 law allowed the Congress to disapprove such extensions. A disapproval would, of course, be subject to the president's veto, and that would be subject to a congressional override.)

One year later, on May 3, 1994, during the annual review of MFN status, President Clinton said, "I do not seek, nor would it be proper, for the United States or any other nation to tell a great nation like China how to conduct all its internal affairs or treat all its citizens, or what laws it should have. That would be wrong." Then, on May 26, 1994, he said that "serious human rights abuses continue in China," but regardless of that he would renew MFN, and that MFN "offers us the best opportunity to lay the basis for long-term sustainable progress on human rights and for the advancement of our other interests with China."

The 103rd Congress approved.

One year later, on May 26, 1995, he renewed MFN status again, this time going even further, saying he was going to "*delink* human rights from the annual extension of Most Favored Nation trading status for China."

The 104th Congress approved.

And so MFN was to continue annually without regard to human rights violations.

The 105th Congress approved.

In June 1995, against the advice of the U.S. State Department, Taiwan's President Lee accepted an invitation from Cornell University to receive its first Outstanding International Alumnus Citation. In retaliation for that journey to the United States, the People's Republic of China launched missile tests in waters near Taiwan and recalled its ambassador to the United States.

The following year was an election year in Taiwan and what concerned the government of the People's Republic of China most was the potential of President Lee being reelected. In an attempt to influence the defeat of an additional term for President Lee, in March 1996, just prior to the elections in Taiwan, the People's Republic of China conducted intensive live-fire exercises off Taiwan by its ships, as well as ground and air exercises in the northwest section of the Taiwan Strait. In addition, the People's Republic of China fired four unarmed surface-to-surface missiles off the coast of two Taiwan ports.

The People's Republic of China warned the United States not to interfere in what was an "internal affair," but President Clinton did not follow the more common and weak procedure of ambiguity. Instead, he sent two aircraft carrier battle groups to the area (two aircraft carriers and thirty-six supporting ships and submarines) but he did not have them sent through the strait itself. His decision of showing the flag in such a large-scale operation proved effective.

The incident was over after Taiwan's election was held. President Lee, who had called the actions of the People's Republic of China "state terrorism," won with 54 percent of the votes. In that 1996 election President Lee became the first *directly* elected president. Previous presidential elections and reelections had been carried out by the National Assembly (started in 1946 on the continent, and through the years in Taiwan retaining its Kuomintang domination) bypassing the idea of direct presidential elections and even bypassing Taiwan's Legislative Yuan (the legislature started by the Kuomintang in 1947–48 in China and retained in Taiwan).

President Lee's victory was not well received in Beijing. A senior People's Liberation Army officer was quoted in the Beijing-backed *Wen Wei Po* newspaper in Hong Kong as saying, "In the future, conducting military exercises on a still greater scale, or adopting other military actions to strike at Taiwanese independence plots, and at foreign forces vainly attempting to obstruct China's reunification, will not be ruled out."

It was not a unique statement; just a new way to put it.

On February 19, 1997, the People's Republic of China's "paramount leader," Deng Xiaoping, died at the age of ninety-two. Although Deng held no official position at the time of his death and Jiang Zemin had already taken over the government's formal leadership, Deng did not need an office to be admired and respected by the government of the People's Republic of China and the U.S. State Department. (In truth he did have a title of sorts as "Bridge Commissioner." This was not to be confused with a commission on bridges that crossed rivers and roads, but a commission dedicated to the card game of bridge.) His monument was the absence of the statue called "The Goddess of Democracy" built and erected in Tiananmen Square by students and smashed to destruction by a tank the dawn of June 5, 1989, while the last of the thousands of bodies from the massacre were being taken away by soldiers.

Deng's legacy was passed on to those who followed him, even to the attempted justification of the Tiananmen Square Massacre in statements made by his successor, President Jiang Zemin and Premier Li Peng (followed later by President Hu Jintao and Premier Wen Jiabo).

In May 1997, President Clinton accused the government of the People's Republic of China of allowing American goods to be pirated and duplicated. It was a valid charge: Chinese companies were producing copies of U.S. films, recordings of music, CDs, and other intellectual property of Americans, violating copyright agreements. With the support of the U.S. business community, President Clinton threatened the People's Republic of China with as much as 100 percent tariff increases if such copyright violations continued. That meant billions of dollars in new tariffs on a host of items imported to the United States from China, including textiles, synthetic fiber apparel, cosmetics, and auto parts.

Under such a threat, the government of the People's Republic of China stopped allowing such internal piracy (at least temporarily) and therefore the increased tariffs did not need to be imposed by the United States. It was a great and noble victory for President Clinton and for the business community.

But in the doing of it, something else was revealed that was *not* great and noble. The president and many in the business community were willing to invoke economic punishments on the People's Republic of China for the violation of copyrights—but not for the violation of human rights.

Profiteers think of China as having more than one billion customers, as is so frequently stated. They should, however, give some thought to China having more than one billion *human beings*, as they so *in*frequently state.

On March 13, 1998, the United States announced it would no longer sponsor a resolution to condemn the human rights violations of the People's Republic of China before the United Nations Commission on Human Rights, as it had every year since the Tiananmen Square Massacre. The resolution had not passed over the years, but the U.S. sponsorship of it was a powerful statement of concern by the people of the United States. Therefore it became an equally powerful statement when the United States discontinued sponsoring that annual attempt. That resolution was one of the only remaining cornerstones of the human rights policy of the United States toward the People's Republic of China.

As a result of the president's refusal to continue U.S. sponsorship, the U.S. Congress voted for a resolution opposing the president's decision. The Senate vote was 95 to 5; the House vote was 397 to 0. (The president can ignore congressional resolutions, as they are nonbinding. It was ignored.)

On June 27, 1998, U.S. President Bill Clinton was greeted in Beijing by President Jiang Zemin at the edge of Tiananmen Square where the massacre took place nine years earlier and in sight of the spot where the Goddess of Democracy had been demolished. Later that day, a seventy-minute news conference was held in Beijing's Great Hall of the People.

It was President Clinton's finest hour. His statements advocating human rights and democracy, and his statements about Tibet, dissidents, and freedom of religion were magnificent.

Regarding the Tiananmen Square Massacre, President Clinton said, "I believe, and the American people believe, that the use of force and the tragic loss of life was wrong." He then said that governments must protect the freedoms of speech, association, and religion, and a pledge to protect these freedoms is a part of the Charter of the United Nations.

President Jiang answered, "Had the Chinese government not taken the resolute measures then, we could not have enjoyed the stability that we are enjoying today."

That attempt of rationalization certainly implied that the government would take the same resolute measures again so as to continue to enjoy stability.

Within the news conference, it was announced with pride by both Presidents Clinton and Jiang that both nations agreed to stop targeting each other with their nuclear-armed missiles. Since retargeting can be accomplished in 58 seconds, this decision was explained as an end to the threat of an accidental nuclear launch. (The CIA had reported earlier that 13 of 18 CSS-4 missiles were targeted on U.S. cities. In 2006 this was revised to 20 intercontinental ballistic missiles "capable of hitting the United States.") It was later learned that during President Clinton's visit, the People's Republic of China test-fired a DF-31 solid-fuel rocket motor that was part of their development of its newest road-mobile solid fueled intercontinental ballistic missile that could hit the United States. The test was carried out about 250 miles southwest of Beijing, at the Wuzhai Missile and Space Test Center. (By 2006 it was estimated that with China's continued DF31 development, a totally mobile force with multiple warheads called the DF31-A, could be deployed by 2007 with intercontinental ballistic missiles launched from trucks or trains.)

By this time, the People's Republic of China was an acknowledged potential superpower. That term has a short but precise history. The United States and the Soviet Union were labeled as the two superpowers during the decades of the Cold War. But the Soviet Union was not a superpower economically or industrially or technologically or agriculturally or morally. The only area in which it was a superpower was militarily—but that made the claim legitimate. That is exactly the status that free countries have been granting to the People's Republic of China, in addition to guaranteeing it will have superpower economic status.

From Beijing, President Clinton went on to visit Shanghai, where on Tuesday, June 30, 1998, he undid the good he had done in Beijing with an unexpected and alarming statement: "We don't support independence for Taiwan, or two Chinas, or one Taiwan and one China. And we don't believe that Taiwan should be a member in any organization for which statehood is a requirement." He was paraphrasing what had long been called "The Three No's" of the People's Republic of China. The wording of President Clinton's statement had been planned in an earlier exchange between his representatives and Vice Foreign Minister Xiang Huaicheng in Xian.

Shortly after President Clinton's trip to China, on July 22, 1998, the Most Favored Nation's name for trade status in the United States was changed to Permanent Normal Trade Relations (PNTR). Many businesspeople were elated. Those were the businesspeople whose overwhelming interests were not in democracy and liberty. Their overwhelming interest was in expanding their financial portfolios, which were larger than their consciences.

The great ancient war strategist of China, Sun-tzu, had said, "Those skilled at making the enemy move do so by creating a situation to which he must conform. They entice him with something he is certain to take and with lures of ostensible profit. They await him in strength."

President Theodore Roosevelt said that if we "sink into a nation of mere hucksters, putting gain over national honor, and subordinating everything to mere ease of life, then we shall indeed reach a condition worse than that of the ancient civilizations in the years of their decay."

There is a book that was written before the U.S. entry into World War II entitled *You Can't Do Business With Hitler* by Douglas Miller and published by Atlantic-Little. The author wrote, "We must get this straight once and for all: there is no such thing as having purely economic relations with the totalitarian states. Every business deal carries with it political, military, social, and propaganda implications." That book was not a best seller. It was ignored by many businesspeople and by many governments selling their wares to Nazi Germany and making deals for profit.

Those things learned by one generation are rarely accepted by succeeding generations. And so each generation has paid another price in human misery.

While there has been expansion in the width of some wallets, those individual financial gains have not been expansive for the United States as a whole. MFN and Permanent Normal Trade Status with the People's Republic of China has brought an average tariff of approximately 4 percent charged by the U.S. on goods from China entering the United States compared to 30–50 percent charged by the PRC for U.S. goods entering China. During the year of 2005 the PRC enjoyed a surplus in trade with the United States of over 200 billion U.S. dollars. By the end of 2005, the PRC's foreign exchange reserves reached 818.9 billion U.S. dollars, with a crossing of the one-trillion-dollar mark expected sometime in the near future.

The moral case for *maintaining* our trade status with China, whether it was called Most Favored Nation status (MFN) or is called Permanent Normal Trade Relations (PNTR), is that constructive engagement will bring the Chinese government closer to our system, encouraging that government to bring about a democratic framework without human rights violations.

The moral case for *rejecting* such a trade status is that slaves are not freed by rewarding their masters. If the Soviet Union's dictatorial system's demise was due in large part to economic failure, why should China's dictatorial system end because of its economic success?

The quest for personal wealth can always be publicly cloaked in some fictitious motivation of serving all humanity. But China's economic growth through trade and the investment of Western nations has brought with it a more than commensurate growth of China's military power—without any force in the world threatening China. It has also brought about a more than commensurate growth in human rights violations in China, making a mockery of humane justifications of traders and investors.

The military policies of the government of the People's Republic of China include expanding its quantity of intercontinental ballistic missiles and the transfer of military technology, including assistance to missile and nuclear programs, for North Korea and Iran and close ties with Cuba, Sudan, Myanmar, and Hugo Chavez of Venezuela.Missile technology and components have gone from China to Iran then on to Syria, where they have been transported to Lebanon for Hezbollah terrorists. Iran's Raad Missile with a range in excess of 300 miles and a warhead of 1,100 pounds is based on the Silkworm Missiles received from China. According to "The National Security and Military/Commercial Concerns with the People's Republic of China Select Committee of the United States House of Representatives", better known as the Christopher Cox Committee, the People's Republic of China sold Iran significant numbers of 90-mile range CSS-8 ballistic missiles, along with associated support and guidance and telemetry components, and also provided assistance to Iran's nuclear weapons program. In contrast, according to the *Taipei Times*, Taiwan gave financial aid in support of U.S. military efforts in Afghanistan and Iraq, volunteered to be part of "The Coalition of the Willing," and offered to send five thousand marines to Iraq. That offer was not accepted. Had it been accepted, the U.S. State Department wouldn't know what to do about it. How would they record it in the list of nations forming the coalition? Since Taiwan is not accepted as a nation by the United States government, would it be recorded in the list as Taiwan (not recognized as its name) or the Republic of China (not recognized as a national government) or a province of the People's Republic of China (as China insists)?

Domestic policies of the People's Republic of China include forced abortions and other penalties for having more than one child, or if divorced and remarried, more than a second child if a new spouse is childless. Penalties beyond a forced abortion can include the withholding of social services, the loss of employment, imprisonment, and even execution. Harry Wu testified to the House of Representatives International Relations Committee that Document 43 of Jieshi Township on August 26, 2003, gave orders that the Autumn 2003 Family Planning Assignment should begin on August 26, and within 35 days the goals must be achieved: to sterilize 1,369, fit 818 with an IUD, induce labor for 108, and carry out 163 abortions. China Reform Monitor #602 told of some 7,000 people being forcibly sterilized between March and July of 2005 in Tinan County of Shandong Province, with relatives who tried to help pregnant women sometimes being beaten to death while in detention.

Catholics are required to register with the "Catholic Patriotic Association"; Protestants are required to register with the "Three Self Patriotic Movement." China has a prison system patterned after the Soviet's Gulag Archipelago, called the Laogai ("reform through labor") with an estimated 1.78 million political prisoners in 1,155 documented prisons. There is a prohibition of Red Cross inspections of those prisons. Their policy includes the selling of organs from executed prisoners. Other practices, offenses, and punishments include the exile or imprisonment or execution of dissidents, with sentences to death for Bible smuggling; the sentence of death for "using a cult (the South China Church) to undermine the enforcement of the law"; the illegality of the Falun Gong practice of exercise and meditation; continued repression of the people of Tibet; the expulsion or execution of over 6,000 Tibetan Monks, and the continued moving of Chinese into Tibet to change the balance of ethnicity so Tibetans become a minority.

China's government continues to defend its support of Pol Pot and his Khmer Rouge of the 1970s, the Tiananmen Square Massacre of the 1980s, and missile sales to rogue states of the 1990s into the twenty-first century.

Any free person who has some interest in what the future could bring would want to influence the People's Republic of China in the direction of democracy. But there are only three publicly exposed ways for one government to influence another: diplomatically, economically, or militarily. Once President Carter gave diplomatic relations to the People's Republic of China, the United States had little left with which to give or hold back on a diplomatic level. Obviously, the military option is the very last one that should be used.

That leaves the economic or middle option and with little exception, there is refusal to use it. Therefore, why should the government of the People's Republic of China release its political prisoners, stop its other violations of human rights, end its military transfers, cut back the continued escalation of its military budget, end its threats against Taiwan, and accept democratic principles? With our continued economic partnership, the PRC's government has found the magic formula in achieving a tremendous economy with the largest army in the world, while retaining its political dictatorship over China's population.

An old Chinese man who, along with Tibetans, walked across the Himalayan Mountains to Darjeeling, India, to escape from China after Mao Tse-tung's communist revolution, repeated what he said was an old Chinese proverb: "Freedom is like oxygen. You don't think about it until it's gone."

Most people of Taiwan are visionary enough to think of that frequently told statement before the gasps for oxygen begin, but one of the great disappointments is that many businesspeople in Taiwan are guilty of ignoring those words. According to *China Daily*, Taiwanese investors have funded 67,714 projects in China. Trade between Taiwan and China reached $82.3 billion by 2004 and reached $93.4 billion by 2005 with almost three billion more added in just the first five months of 2006, with Taiwan being China's fourth largest investor. China is Taiwan's largest export market, responsible for 37.7 percent of all Taiwan's exports in 2005. At the end of 2005, an estimated one million Taiwanese businesspeople were living in China. All of this can lead to Taiwan's economic reliance on such links, creating a risk that Taiwan will not be independent but dependent on China.

For a quick profit, those businesspeople risk the freedom of Taiwan's next generation. The risk they face, although they don't think of it this way, is that they are selling the liberty of their own children.

For sure, greed is a contagious disease that has gone well beyond national boundaries. Admittedly, the greed of individuals is controlled under dictatorships, but in free countries there is no vaccination to bring about immunization from such immoral temptation. And so there remains an increasing avalanche of trading and investment in the People's Republic of China, endangering the freedom of those who have it and endangering the lives of those who don't.

CHAPTER EIGHT

ALWAYS BY THE NUMBERS

SINCE IT BEGAN in 1949, the government of the People's Republic of China has suffered under the disability of three obsessions:

1. The lust for governmental control.

2. The policy that China's treaties and agreements made prior to the communist revolution have no continuing authority, while any territory they regard as a possession during pre-revolution China must obey China's current authority.

3. The belief that China's unelected government is superior to giving the choice of leaders to those governed: the people of China or the people of any place they consider to be part of China.

After Great Britain's 1997 handover of Hong Kong to the government of the People's Republic of China and, to a lesser extent Portugal's 1999 handover of Macau to the PRC government, all three obsessions have been targeted at Taiwan for which the PRC has long proclaimed what they call "The Three No's":

1. No independence of Taiwan.

2. No acceptance of diplomatic relations with any government that proclaims there are two Chinas, or one China and one Taiwan.

3. No acceptance of Taiwan into any international organization as a separate state.

Those "Three No's," having been paraphrased by U.S. presidents, placed U.S. policy in an untenable position, seeming to *accept* the position that Taiwan was nothing other than the "renegade province" of the PRC.

On July 9, 1999, President Lee of Taiwan used three words that created a firestorm. In a radio interview with *Deutsche Welle* ("Voice of Germany") President Lee said that any talks between China and Taiwan should be conducted on a "state-to-state" relationship.

The People's Republic of China quickly warned of military intervention against Taiwan. The Clinton administration in the U.S. was up in arms over President Lee's statement, and President Lee's political party, the Kuomintang, made futile attempts to soften what President Lee had said.

The PRC's minister of defense, Chi Haotian, said that the army "is ready at any time to safeguard the territorial integrity of China and smash any attempts to separate the country."

President Clinton phoned China's president Jiang Zemin to assure him that the United States retained a "one China" policy.

The spokesman for the Ministry of Foreign Affairs in Beijing, Zhu Bangzao, said, "We hereby warn Lee Teng-hui and the Taiwan authorities not to underestimate the firm resolve of the Chinese government to safeguard the sovereignty, dignity, and territorial integrity of the courage and strength of the Chinese people to fight against separation and Taiwan's independence. The reunification of China represents the general trend and the popular will. Lee Teng-hui and Taiwan authorities should size up the situation soberly, rein in at the brink of the precipice, and immediately cease all separatist activities."

Beyond threats, the People's Republic of China used the weapon of international humiliation against Taiwan. Beijing has pressured the World Trade Organization not to give any official titles to representatives from Taiwan, and insists that the World Trade Organization's directory refer to them only as "Mr." and "Ms." rather than any national title. Taiwan wanted to join the Association of Southeast Asian Nations (ASEAN) and was invited to join in 1991 with a precondition stipulated by Beijing. Its membership had to be under the name of Chinese Taipei or it would be unable to join. In order to participate in the Olympic Games, the same designation of Chinese Taipei is required, with the rule that Taiwan cannot have its national anthem played, nor is the display of Taiwan's flag permitted.

President Lee Teng-hui split from the Kuomintang political party in 2000 as the Kuomintang was changing policies toward the People's Republic of China into closer relationships, increased trade, acceptance of humiliations, and pacifying statements. President Lee warned the Kuomintang that their extended hand would eventually be turned into aggression against Taiwan by China.

The Democratic Progressive Party (DPP) that had been born illegally in 1986 expanded in popularity and won the presidential vote of 2000 with the election of President Chen Shui-bian and Vice President Annette Hsiu-lien Lu. For the first time since China reclaimed Taiwan after World War II (held by Japan since 1895), the Kuomintang was out of presidential power.

With the increase of Taiwan's impetus toward formal independence, the People's Republic of China announced a warning of what it called "The Three If's." China would use force:

1. If Taiwan declared independence.

2. If Taiwan was occupied by a foreign power.

3. If Taiwan postponed "reunification" negotiations.

In his inaugural address of 2000, President Chen said what came to be known as "Chen's Four No's" (sometimes referred to as "Chen's Four No's and One Without" or "Chen's Five No's"):

"As long as the CCP [Chinese Communist Party] regime has no intention to use military force against Taiwan,

1. "I pledge that during my term in office I will not declare independence;

2. "I will not change the national title;

3. "I will not push forth the inclusion of the 'state-to-state' description in the Constitution; and

4. "I will not promote a referendum to change the status quo in regard to the question of independence or unification.

The One Without: "Furthermore, the abolition of the National Unification Council or the National Reunification Guidelines will not be an issue."

Throughout the history of most democracies, inaugural addresses have been used to proclaim what the new leader planned on doing—not what the new leader planned on not doing. President Chen's proclamation of what he would not do exhibited that policies were being made from a standpoint of fear. His speech given on his first day in office as president veered sharply away from the speeches of his election campaign. He was now becoming dependent on pleasing President Jiang Zemin, who was targeting Taiwan with missiles, and pleasing President Clinton, who had given his version of the "Three No's," and called the PRC "the strategic partner of the United States."

If Taiwan seeks permission from others for decisions that should be its own, it is *not* independent. Such fear of other national leaders by President Chen was accepted as understandable by some, but his inaugural address was a huge disappointment to many who had the courage to reject fear as the basis of policy. It was particularly disappointing to former president Lee.

Under severe pressure from his own party, President Chen later amended his "Four No's" (or whatever anyone wanted to call them). He said the current reality is that "Taiwan and China [are] standing on opposite sides of the Strait, one *country* on each side."

And he went further. Toward the end of his first term he advocated a referendum, asking the people of Taiwan two questions:

1. The people of Taiwan demand that the Taiwan issue be resolved through peaceful means. Should Mainland China refuse to withdraw the missiles it has targeted at Taiwan and to openly renounce the use of force against us, would you agree that the Government should acquire more advanced anti-missile systems to strengthen Taiwan's self-defense capabilities?

2. Would you agree that our Government should engage
    in negotiations with Mainland China on the establish-
    ment of a "peace and stability" framework for cross-
    strait interactions in order to build consensus and for
    the welfare of the peoples on both sides?

In 2003 his two questions became part of the following year's
calendar. President Chen announced that both questions were to be
asked of the people during the presidential election of 2004. China
protested, claiming such a plebiscite would be an overture to a formal declaration of independence. The United States also opposed
the referendum.

President Chen did not give in.

In the year 2003 Hu Jintao became president of China. His cre-
dentials apparently qualified him: he had been the communist chief
in Tibet who cracked down heavily on dissidents in Lhasa. In 1989 he
was the first regional secretary to send a congratulatory telegram to
the central government following the Tiananmen Square Massacre.

Wen Jiabo became Hu Jintao's premier. Premier Wen was invited
to Washington, D.C., his visit scheduled for December 7–10, 2003.
Days before his visit, on December 3, Chinese State Media reported
that military officials repeated that China would wage war against
the "renegade province"—Taiwan—if it declared independence.

Citizens of Taiwan who endorse the status quo and oppose independence generally give the same answer when asked why they
feel that way: "Any change in the status quo, particularly a proclamation of independence, would mean war. The PRC would attack."
In short, the weapon of fear has already attacked Taiwan.

On December 9, 2003, during Premier Wen Jiabo's visit to
Washington, D.C., President George W. Bush and Premier Wen of
the PRC held a joint news conference. In reference to Taiwan's
scheduled referendum to come in Taiwan, President Bush said: "We
oppose any unilateral decision by either China or Taiwan to change
the status quo. And the comments and actions made by the leader
of Taiwan indicate that he may be willing to make decisions unilaterally that change the status quo. And we oppose that."

Premier Wen answered, "We very much appreciate the position adopted by President Bush towards the latest news and developments in Taiwan; that is the attempt to resort to referendum of various kinds as excuse to pursue Taiwan independence."

How could the United States oppose a democratic government asking its people through a referendum if they would endorse a proposed policy of that government? Just weeks before the Bush-Wen meeting, President Bush had said, "When India's democracy was imperiled in the 1970s, the Indian people showed their commitment to liberty in a national referendum that saved their form of government."

On the day President Bush made his anti-referendum statement to Chinese Premier Wen Jiabo, a senior administration official added that in private discussions, President Bush had told Premier Wen that the United States would intervene on behalf of Taiwan should China use force against Taiwan. The senior administration official added: "I want to stress here that the president's top goal is preserving the peace in the Taiwan Strait. We are in no way abandoning support for Taiwan's democracy or for the spread of freedom. If they try to use force or coercion against the Taiwanese, we're going to be there."

A senior State Department official put it differently than the senior administration official. The senior State Department official said, "We've been forced to react to steps taken by President Chen that seem to be pointing toward independence."

In 2004 former president Lee campaigned for President Chen Shui-bian and Vice President Annette Hsiu-lien Lu, and against his former party, the Kuomintang. Former president Lee had become "the Spiritual Leader" of a new pro-independence party, the "Taiwan Solidarity Union" (TSU).

The political parties that leaned in varied degrees toward formal sovereignty as an independent state were called "Pan-Green" in the Taiwanese vocabulary, while those that leaned toward opposition of independence were called "Pan-Blue." The names expressed two pans (like pans of earth or water being shaken to find gold nuggets or dust) each having their coalition of political parties in either Pan-Green or Pan-Blue. The major Pan-Green parties were the Democratic

Progressive Party (DPP), the Taiwan Solidarity Union (TSU), and the Taiwan Independence Party (TAIP). The major Pan-Blue parties were the old Kuomintang Party (KMT) of the late Chiang Kai-shek, the People First Party (PFP), and the New Party (NP).

On election day in Taiwan, March 20, 2004, Pan-Green was the winner. President Chen and Vice President Lu were reelected, but only by 50.11 percent of the votes cast. The controversial referendum was held as part of that election process. As stated (in their entirety earlier in this chapter), the questions asked the voters if they wanted more anti-missile defenses if the PRC refused to withdraw their missiles aimed at Taiwan and refused to renounce the use of force against Taiwan, and if Taiwan should negotiate with the PRC to establish a peaceful and stable framework for interaction. Eighty-seven percent of the voters checked "yes" to both questions, but the referenda did not become law because the rules of the process stated there had to be participation of at least 50 percent plus one registered voters, and there was participation of 45 percent of registered voters.

President Chen's second inaugural address was another disappointment to many of his supporters when he stated, "Today I would like to reaffirm the promises and principles set forth in my inaugural speech in 2000. Those commitments have been honored— they have not changed over the past four years, nor will they change in the next four years."

On October 25, 2004, U.S. Secretary of State Colin Powell said in an interview with Hong Kong's Phoenix TV, "Taiwan is not independent. It does not enjoy sovereignty as a nation, and that remains our policy; our firm policy." The same day he told CNN International, "We want to see both sides not take unilateral action that would prejudice an eventual outcome; a reunification that all parties are seeking." It was later corrected that the secretary did not mean to say "reunification."

The requirements of an independent nation by the Convention and Rights and Duties of States (December 26, 1933) mandate that such a political entity must have a defined territory, a permanent population, a government, and the capability of entering into relations with other states. All of those requirements have been met by Taiwan. Moreover, in 2005, Taiwan had a population of 23 million people, which was a greater population than almost three-quarters of individual nations in the U.N. in 2005. (140 out of 191 countries).

It was obvious but not admitted by most nations of the world, including the United States, that Taiwan now existed under "The Three Realities":

1. The old ambition of taking over China is done and gone.

2. Taiwan is a true democracy with all democratic foundations including freedom of speech, freedom of the press, freedom of religion, freedom of assembly, freedom to petition the government, a separate legislature from the executive, a separate judiciary from other branches of government, and free, fair, and frequent multi-party elections.

3. Taiwan is a sovereign nation whose democracy is caught in a tightening vice.

From the beginning of June, 2004, just prior to the fifteenth anniversary of the Tiananmen Square Massacre, President Hu Jintao ordered that family members of people killed during that massacre should be held under detention (obviously to prevent anniversary protests). His premier, Wen Jiabo, said, "At the end of the 1980s and the beginning of the 1990s, China faced a very serious political disturbance. What hung in the balance was the future of our party and our country. We successfully stabilized the situation of reform and opened up the path of building socialism with Chinese characteristics. These achievements are self-evident for all. Unity and stability are more important than anything else."

He knew there were many around the world who would understand.

December 2004 brought ominous news to Taiwan: the European Union (EU) announced it would work to bring about the end of the embargo of arms and technology to the People's Republic of China.

That embargo had been in effect since the Tiananmen Square Massacre, in protest of that massacre. To end the embargo without any apologies or even regrets by the PRC for what was done in Tiananmen Square, without release of their political prisoners, without any changes in what they continued to do against their own citizens, was a loud statement to the PRC that the European Union didn't want China's political policies to continue to interfere with their own economic pursuits. The timeline presented by the EU was that the embargo would be ended within the next six months. Leading that effort were two European leaders of the time: President Jacque Chirac of France and Chancellor Gerhard Schroeder of Germany.

It could mean a lot of money.

CHAPTER NINE

NAME CHANGE

ONE DAY IN 1949 the people of the Republic of China awoke to find the name of their nation had been changed to the People's Republic of China.

One day in 1975 the people of the Republic of Vietnam awoke to find the name of their nation had been changed to the Socialist Republic of Vietnam.

One day in 1984 the people of Upper Volta awoke to find the name of their nation had been changed to Burkina Faso.

One day in 1989 the people of Burma awoke to find the name of their nation had been changed to Myanmar.

Those name changes were made by governments that had taken over the peoples of those countries by force.

History is full of nations that have undergone name changes by force. But in current years the policy of most governments of the world is to deny the *elected* government of the Republic of China on Taiwan to call for a *referendum* that would give the people the *choice* of retaining their name of the Republic of China or changing it to Taiwan.

Are nations of the world claiming that name changes that came about through force may be regrettable but acceptable, while a change of name by a free people (23 million free people) making their choice of a name change is unacceptable?

Their answer, of course, is that Taiwan is not a nation but a "renegade province" of the People's Republic of China. And this introduces one of the most absurd ironies of geopolitical history by asking, "Who wants what name when?"

In 1945 when World War II was over and Japan surrendered its jurisdiction of Taiwan, the island was reclaimed by China and the flag of the Republic of China was raised over Taiwan (although, as recorded earlier, Japan did not designate any particular power to have jurisdiction over Taiwan). In 1949, when over one million Chinese led by Chiang Kai-shek fled Mao Tse-tung's communist revolution and went ninety-five miles across the Taiwan Strait to Taiwan, those Chinese refugees continued to observe the flag of the Republic of China that the refugee government had known since 1911 on the continent. But China was now the People's Republic of China and the position of Mao Tse-tung's new Chinese government on the continent was that the old name of the Republic of China was never to be used anywhere. Since the People's Republic of China regarded Taiwan as its property, they wanted it to be known as nothing other than a province of China called Taiwan or Formosa.

Near the beginning of the twenty-first century everything regarding the name reversed.

The name of the nation printed on the passports of those who were citizens of the Republic of China on Taiwan had been "Republic of China." On the first day of September, 2003, Taiwan's minister of foreign affairs, Eugene Chien, started issuing a new passport for Taiwan citizens. On the cover in gold letters is "Republic of China" in Chinese, and below that are the words "Republic of China" in English. Below that is the ROC symbol of a sun with twelve points, and below that is the name "Taiwan" in English. Below all of that is the word "Passport." This created a furor by the government of the People's Republic of China.

The government of the People's Republic of China has come to insist that Taiwan continue to call itself the Republic of China without even a hint of a name change to Taiwan. Logic (rarely a factor in the People's Republic of China's reasoning) would seem to dictate that since the Republic of China was the governmental enemy that fought against the communist revolution, retaining the name of the Republic of China would indicate there was every intention by that government to come back and destroy the government of the People's Republic. That's what it used to mean.

Taiwan's president Chen Shui-bian has continually stated that he would not call for a formal change of the name of the Republic of China to Taiwan, but that he does want to end the confusion among many throughout the world who do not know whether they are dealing with the Beijing government or the Taipei government because the name "China" is used by both governments. President Chen has advocated changing the name of his government's foreign missions in host nations and changing the name of state enterprises such as "China Airlines," "China Steel," "China Ship Building," and "China Petroleum," and stating they should at least have the word "Taiwan" as part of their names to avoid the very frequent confusion of those who think the names signify they are establishments of the People's Republic of China.

Although the U.S. State Department did not give any support or opposition to the change on the cover of Taiwan's passport as "nothing to do with the United States," the U.S. State Department's deputy spokesman, Adam Ereli, said, "These changes of terminology for government-controlled enterprises or economic and cultural offices abroad, in our view, would appear to unilaterally change Taiwan's status, and for that reason we are not supportive of them."

Not asked of Adam Ereli or addressed by him was a larger, more positive element that would be achieved by a name change from the Republic of China to Taiwan: it would be a formal statement to the international community that Taiwan does not want "two Chinas." It would be a formal statement that Taiwan acknowledges there is only one China with the People's Republic as its government. Taiwan, no longer claiming China, therefore no longer wants the name of the Republic of China because there cannot be two Chinas. Since the international community, including the United States, stresses a "one China" policy, such a name should be celebrated. But it isn't.

In August of 2005 an exhibition at the U.N. for its sixtieth anniversary displayed a poster with the names of the 51 nations that signed the U.N. Charter in 1945, the poster titled "Original Signatories of the U.N. Charter." They included the name of "China, People's Republic of" which, of course, didn't even exist then and was certainly not one of its signers in 1945, and not even given membership in the U.N. until 1971. The Republic of China's name was missing on the U.N. poster although it was not only one of the 51 signers of the Charter in 1945, but was one of the five founding nations.

Adding to the absurdity of the conflict regarding the name, since 1993, Taiwan's government has made an annual effort to re-enter the United Nations, not at the expense of the membership of the People's Republic of China, but in addition to it. Starting this effort was President Lee Teng-hui, using the name "Republic of China on Taiwan." The next president, Chen Shui-bian, retained the advocacy for membership in the U.N., changing the name to "Republic of China (Taiwan)." For the fourteenth attempt in 2006, President Chen proposed using the name "Taiwan." A poll of 1,072 people in Taiwan conducted by the private "Taiwan Thinktank" concluded that 79 percent of the respondents wanted the name of "Taiwan" to be used in the fourteenth attempt to regain membership in the United Nations. On September 12, 2006, the U.N. wouldn't even allow the submitted question of "the representation and participation of the 23 million people of Taiwan in the United Nations" to be part of the U.N. agenda.

Regardless of the name chosen, the attempt has so far been futile. Short of a miracle or a total political and moral change in either the U.N. or China, Taiwan's attempt to get back into the U.N. will not be successful, having been kicked out of that failed international organization in 1971. In truth, it is an honor to be kicked out of the U.N. (the United States should have that good luck) and Taiwan should never humiliate itself by trying to get back into an organization from which it was ejected.

In view of Taiwan's problems with national identity, the name—although the most important element—is not the only element. Taiwan's Trong Chai, a Democratic Progressive Party lawmaker, wants to amend Article Two of the Constitution to read, "The national emblem of the Republic of China shall be determined in a referendum. The Ministry of Interior shall advertise for designs and decide how the same designs should be collected...It should display the spirit of Taiwan's love for peace and freedom, emphasize Taiwan's independent identity as well as its history and culture, and differ from any of those of other nations...[It] shall not be the same as or similar to any of those of political parties in our country." (That was added because the emblem of the nation and the emblem of the Kuomintang Party are practically one and the same, both having been established by the Kuomintang.)

On June 7, 2005, Taiwan's National Assembly, making the requirements for constitutional change, approved standards for any constitutional amendment or changes in the future—but not for the best. The changes were obviously meant to pacify both the People's Republic of China and the United States, setting requirements unlikely to be achieved: changes could only come about if three-fourths of the legislature passes an amendment, and then in a national referendum the amendment receives 50 percent (plus one) of the approval of all *eligible* voters rather than 50 percent (plus one) of all those *voting*.

Originally, the members of the National Assembly acted under Chiang Kai-shek when he was president of China. Its purpose was to be an electoral college, electing the president and vice president and to make changes in the constitution. He brought the members with him to Taiwan in 1949 where that assembly was referred to by many as the "eternal parliament" and the "old thieves" with its members retained. Those who remember and recorded it say it started with 3,045 members, but their power kept diminishing as democracy was taking hold. In the mid- and late 1980s and through the 1990s more than half of the original members were dead or retired, some replaced with new members. There were 780 members in 2000 not knowing quite what to do since real legislative power had been given to the elected Taiwan Legislative Yuan (a congress) and the Control Yuan (designed to confirm presidential nominees and serve as a watchdog agency with the power of recommending impeachment or censure of executive branch officials). Additionally, the National Assembly no longer had the power to decide who would be president, as that power had been replaced by direct elections of the people. The National Assembly disbanded that year. It was then reinstated later in 2000 and again in 2005 with a comparatively mere three hundred delegates, its 2005 reinstatement made for only two purposes: to set the procedure for constitutional changes without them, and to abolish itself for good. The National Assembly committed suicide in 2005.

No flowers requested or received.

CHAPTER TEN

CONQUEST ENTERED INTO LAW

THE YEAR 2005 began in political roars from across the Taiwan Strait.

At the insistence of the People's Republic of China, Taiwan was denied admission to the Tsunami-Aid Summit in Jakarta. It was also excluded from lists of contributing nations in major publications around the world. Taiwan (untouched by the tsunami) was the eighteenth largest tsunami-aid contributor of the nations of the world.

All of this was happening while the People's Republic of China announced it was preparing an "Anti-Secession Bill" that would soon go through the National People's Congress, its intention being to codify the long-held statements of the PRC's leaders: if formal independence was ever declared by Taiwan, the PRC would not hesitate to go to war.

In response came a surprising and uplifting event for Taiwan. The acting secretary general of Japan's ruling party said that "it would be wrong for us to send a signal to China that the United States and Japan will watch and tolerate China's military invasion of Taiwan." On Sunday, February 20, a U.S.–Japan Joint Agreement was announced, stating that security in the Taiwan Strait "is a common strategic objective."

On Sunday, March 13, one day before the scheduled passage of the Anti-Secession Bill, President Hu Jintao said: "We shall step up preparations for possible military struggle and enhance our capabilities to cope with crisis, safeguard peace, prevent wars, and win the wars if any."

Since there is no opposition party in China, the vote in the National People's Congress on Monday, March 14, 2005, was not surprising; 2,896 voted for the pending bill with two abstentions and none against it. Equally unsurprising was that immediately after the "vote," the bill was signed by President Hu Jintao.

There were ten articles to the bill, all of them regarding Taiwan, but its reason for being was summed up in Article 8: "In the event that the 'Taiwan Independence' secessionist forces should act under any name or by any means to cause the fact of Taiwan's secession from China, or that major incidents entailing Taiwan's secession from China should occur, or that possibilities for a peaceful reunification should be completely exhausted, the state shall employ non-peaceful means and other necessary measures to protect China's sovereignty and territorial integrity.

"The State Council and the Central Military Commission shall decide on and execute the non-peaceful means and other necessary measures as provided for in the preceding paragraph and shall promptly report to the Standing Committee of the National People's Congress."

But neither the 23 million people of Taiwan nor its leaders had any plan to secede from a nation of which they were not a part.

The statements from the People's Republic of China continued, each one containing a warning, generally following Hu Jintao's repeated use of the term espousing "territorial integrity," meaning Taiwan is part of China. It became the code phrase for "non-peaceful means."

Russian president Vladimir Putin offered his opinion, which appeared to have been lifted from Hu Jintao's statements. "The Soviet Union and Russia have always been in favor of China's territorial integrity. We have not changed our position and think that China has a right to fully restore its territorial integrity."

White House press secretary Scott McClellan used the State Department's cherished word "stability" but at least he didn't use Hu's and Putin's term of "territorial integrity": "We view the adoption of the Anti-Secession Law as unfortunate. It does not serve the purpose of peace and stability in the Taiwan Strait." It wasn't much of a statement.

In fairness, his statement was by *far* better than the one offered by State Department spokesman Richard Boucher just six days before the law was passed with the certain knowledge that passage was scheduled for the coming Monday: "Our policy, I think, is well-known. But let me say again, we're committed to a 'one China' policy; we uphold the three communiqués. We do not support Taiwan independence. Moreover we oppose any attempts to unilaterally alter the status quo by either side. We'll continue to talk to both sides about these developments. We'll continue to urge both sides to avoid steps that raise tension, that risk beginning a cycle of reaction and counter-action."

Two days after the PRC's Anti-Secession Bill became law, the U.S. House of Representatives passed a resolution condemning it, stating the passage of that law changed "the status quo in the region and thus is of grave concern to the United States." It further stated that the future of Taiwan should be resolved by peaceful means with the consent of the people of Taiwan. (How would their consent be gauged if, as U.S. policy dictated, a referendum should not be held?)

The People's Republic of China reacted with anger at the House resolution. An unnamed spokesman for the Chinese legislature (but officially quoted by the PRC's Xinhua News Agency) announced, "While the U.S. House of Representatives disregarded facts and passed a resolution blaming China for changing the status quo, it totally confused right and wrong...No foreign forces have the right to intervene."

Sun Yafu, deputy director of Beijing's Taiwan Affairs Office of the State Council said, "In the coming three years, if war breaks out across the Taiwan Straits, there would be only one possibility; that is the Taiwan independence secessionist forces misjudge the situation and thus rush recklessly into danger."

Unexpected benefits to Taiwan started to pour in from other nations of the world. Under pressure from President Bush, combined with the passage of the PRC's Anti-Secession Law and the reaction to it by the U.S. House of Representatives, the European Union's planned termination of the arms and technology embargo of China was now in doubt. Great Britain and Sweden were particularly outspoken in their opposition to lifting the embargo. It was also not lost on European leaders that President Bush had made a statement against the EU's original plan in words the State Department had never used: he warned that the transfer of weapons and technology "would change the balance of relations between China and Taiwan." It may not seem to be as meaningful as it was but the president spoke of China and Taiwan as two separate entities. In the halls of foreign ministries that did not go unnoticed. The expected ambiguity would have indicated a statement without using names, stating that the end of the embargo "could increase tensions on both sides of the Taiwan Strait."

Even clearer was another warning by President Bush: if Europe ended its embargo of weapons and technology to the People's Republic of China it could "bring to Asia, the weapons of Europe being opposite the weapons of the United States."

A demonstration was scheduled to take place in Taipei to protest Beijing's Anti-Secession Law. As soon as the announcement of a pending demonstration in Taiwan was made, there was an appeal from Beijing as published by their Xinhua News Agency: "Scholars of the Research Center of Cross-Strait Relations have called on Taiwan residents not to participate in secessionist activities. The call came when a few Taiwan secessionists planned to hold protests against the recently adopted Anti-Secessionist Law on this coming Saturday, March 26. At a meeting in Beijing, the scholars say they hope Taiwan residents understand the law and do not listen to separatist forces."

Saturday's demonstration was neither cancelled nor postponed. The demonstration was held by an estimated one million Taiwan residents through the streets of Taipei. A boom on a truck was used to cover street signs named after cities in China, replacing them with new street signs that represented the thrust of the demonstration. The street sign "Ningpo West Street" was covered with a sign that read "Democracy Road." The sign of "Nanchang City" was covered with a sign reading "Freedom Road."

The demonstrators came in ten different processions, coming together in front of the Presidential Palace where they were greeted by President Chen as they chanted and shouted, "Protect democracy. Love peace. Defend Taiwan." In front of President Chen was a sea of people waving flags of Taiwan along with flags of the United States and Japan in recognition of the new U.S.–Japan Joint Agreement that called for security in the Taiwan Strait as a common strategic objective.

Former President Lee Teng-hui joined the demonstration in solidarity. Songs were sung, most prominently, "We Shall Overcome" and "Blowin' in the Wind." President Chen joined the demonstrators in the singing of "Taiwan Is Our Baby."

He did not give a speech.

A prayer was given at the end of the march. "We will never give up the right to determine our own future. It is a right neither we nor our offspring will give up. We hope the 1.3 billion friendly people of China can enjoy the same democracy, liberty, and freedom from fear as we do...We hope people with like minds will join us in our prayer. May God bless Taiwan, both its people and its land."

In China, BBC and CNN broadcasts (only allowed to be seen at select hotels and some other facilities reserved for foreigners) had their transmissions blacked out as those networks covered the demonstration. Chinese newspapers did not print pictures of the demonstrators.

The one sour note in Taiwan that day was an important one: representatives from the Kuomintang political party did not participate in the demonstration.

It was a sign of coming events.

Although the Kuomintang stayed away from the streets of Taipei on that Saturday, some of their leaders planned to be on the streets of Beijing on Wednesday.

Two days after the demonstration, Chiang Pin-kung, vice chairman of the Kuomintang Party, left Taipei with a twenty-seven-member delegation for a five-day visit to the People's Republic of China. The trip, the first of any Taiwan party leader since the war that ended in 1949, included stops in Guangzhou and the former

Republic of China's capital of Nanjing, with the major destination being the current capital of the People's Republic of China: Beijing.

Although they fought a war against each other, both the Kuomintang and the government of the PRC found mutual agreement in opposing independence for Taiwan.

Taiwan's Chiang Pin-kung said on arrival in China, "We oppose Taiwan independence. We advocate peace across the Strait and oppose the mainland using force."

The Kuomintang delegation and the PRC agreed on a list of ten proposals, most dealing with economic links between China and Taiwan, including the opening of China's financial market. By virtue of Taiwan's laws that prohibit political parties from making international agreements, and since the Kuomintang no longer represented the government of Taiwan, the signatures on the papers meant nothing. Similar to and more stringent than the Logan Act of the United States, Taiwan's Article 113 of their Criminal Code bans unauthorized political parties and private citizens from negotiating agreements with foreign governments under risk of being charged with treason. Chen Chuei, a spokesman for the prosecutor's office of Taiwan's High Court, said the government "is investigating whether the KMT has violated the criminal code, which stipulates against reaching an agreement with any foreign government without authorization."

At the urging of the vice chairman of the Kuomintang Party, Chiang Pin-kung, officials of the PRC extended an invitation to the Kuomintang's chairman, Lien Chan, to visit Beijing. An invitation was also offered to Chairman James Soong of the other major Pan-Blue party, the People First Party (PFP).

On the Pan-Green side, former Taiwan president Lee Teng-hui addressed a rally of a hundred Taiwan Native Civic Groups who banded together to form what was called a "Hand in Hand to Protect Taiwan Alliance." Before he spoke there were chants of "Lien-Soong Sell Out Taiwan!" There was then a reading of a statement saying the visits to China "create the false impression to international society that the Taiwan people accepted the Anti-Secession Law...100 Taiwan native civic groups defend Taiwan's sovereignty and fiercely oppose Lien Chan, James Soong, and other politicians from uniting with the PRC and selling out Taiwan."

Former president Lee warned that the visits to China would eliminate the impact of the "3/26 March for Peace and Democracy to Protect Taiwan" against the PRC's Anti-Secession Law. He demanded that the Democratic Progressive Party government, and particularly the man he had supported, President Chen Shui-bian, "stiffen up" and act to display public authority.

CHAPTER ELEVEN

THE OFFER OF ONE COUNTRY, TWO SYSTEMS

BACK ON MAY 11, 1998, the Central Committee of the Chinese Communist Party started a three-day conference regarding Taiwan with the attendance of members of the Chinese Communist Party's Politburo, including President Jiang Zemin. It was the first time such a meeting took place to exclusively discuss the Taiwan issue. The conclusion was summed up by a statement advocating a "One Country, Two Systems" solution for Taiwan, as Hong Kong had since July 1, 1997, and Macau would have starting December 20, 1999.

The chairman of Taiwan's Mainland Affairs Council, Chang King-yuh, responded from Taiwan that "any arrangement that would downgrade us to a local government will not be acceptable to us." President Lee said that such a policy would be "totally contradictory to the concept of democracy."

Since July 1, 1997, Hong Kong has lived under the concept of "one country, two systems"" as an SAR, standing for "Special Administrative Region" of the People's Republic of China. (Notice that it does not stand for a "Special Autonomous Region" since the term "Tibet Autonomous Region" was used for Tibet, and the world learned in short time there was no autonomy involved.)

In order to have jurisdiction over all of Hong Kong in 1997, the People's Republic of China had to break two agreements (cited earlier) signed by China before there was a PRC. What we call Hong Kong is, in reality, three entities, and two of those entities were given in *perpetuity* to Great Britain. The two entities given *forever* were Hong Kong Island, and across the harbor from the island, the Kowloon peninsula on the continent. The third entity was north of

Kowloon, called the New Territories. Even though in 1841 Hong Kong Island was ceded over from China to Great Britain *in perpetuity*, and a treaty of 1860 gave Kowloon to Great Britain *in perpetuity*, the New Territories were only *leased*, not ceded, to Great Britain. That lease was signed in 1898 to last a period of 99 years for expiration in 1997.

As the years went on, those three entities—Hong Kong Island, Kowloon, and the New Territories—became internationally known as one political structure called Hong Kong. If nothing else, brevity demanded it as all three were under Great Britain's jurisdiction with only the third entity granted on lease.

The 1997 fate of all three entities was sealed in a heated September 1982 meeting in Beijing between Great Britain's prime minister Margaret Thatcher and the leader of the People's Republic of China, Deng Xiaoping. Despite Prime Minister Thatcher's arguments, Deng demanded that Great Britain hand over all three entities—Hong Kong Island, Kowloon, and the New Territories—to the People's Republic of China on July 1, 1997. In protest, Prime Minister Thatcher presented the fact that Hong Kong Island and Kowloon were given to Great Britain in perpetuity by China. Deng Xiaoping wrote those two treaties off as being "unequal treaties" and China would take all the entities come July 1, 1997.

Prime Minister Thatcher's only victory was that Deng agreed to allow Hong Kong to retain its own system for the next fifty years, until 2047. "One Country, Two Systems" was the way he defined it. The error of that definition was that the two systems were decreed as communism for the mainland and capitalism for Hong Kong. But the system of the mainland was fascism and the system of Hong Kong was liberty. On the mainland of China, most large urban areas were highly capitalistic at the time of handover—but the people did not live in liberty. Capitalism is nothing more or less than the economic dimension of liberty, but not the only element. It is for sure that a people cannot be free without capitalism, but it is possible to have capitalism and not be free, as has been proven by so many fascist governments. And that is just the way the government of the People's Republic of China wants it: a dictatorship that exalts one party, one government, and one race.

1997

And so it happened, and the phrase "One Country, Two Systems" was inaugurated in Hong Kong on the midnight that separated June the 30th from July the First of 1997.

Prior to the prescribed handover, Tung Chee-hwa was "elected" Hong Kong's chief executive to take office for five years starting at the moment of jurisdiction by the People's Republic of China. His election was decided by an Election Committee of four hundred who were chosen by the Preparatory Committee, which was chosen by Beijing.

On handover night, Jiang Zemin, the president of the People's Republic of China talked of the shame and humiliation that China had suffered because of the Opium Wars and Great Britain's jurisdiction of Hong Kong for so many years. However, the real humiliation suffered by Jiang Zemin was the evidence on constant display to the world of what Chinese people could do without the government of the People's Republic of China. There was no contest between Hong Kong and any city under the domination of the People's Republic. The shame and humiliation was due to the success of the Chinese people who fled to Hong Kong, rejecting the government of the People's Republic of China.

During that evening, political cracks appeared in the foundation of Hong Kong. Since then, those cracks have widened and deepened and spread further apart.

A convoy of 4,800 soldiers from the People's Liberation Army drove into Hong Kong on handover night with twenty-one anti-riot vehicles. If nothing else, that was a signal to Hong Kong people.

Miles from the border, on Hong Kong Island at the new extension of the Convention and Exhibition Centre, leaders and celebrities from forty-four countries were present, covered by 6,500 media representatives. The handover ceremony was telecast throughout the world. The toast between Jiang Zemin and the Beijing-appointed chief executive of Hong Kong, Tung Chee-hwa, was to Hong Kong's continued prosperity and stability. In the most libertarian enclave on the planet, there was no mention of liberty by its new leaders.

What was not part of the midnight ceremony was any mention of the changes in the laws that governed Hong Kong; the changes coming from "one country, two systems." Those changes (recorded here from personal experiences in Hong Kong during the recorded years and/or from Hong Kong and other international reports during those times) are worthy of notice by the advocates of the People's Republic of China's offer to Taiwan:

1. On June 30 Hong Kong's Bill of Rights was in full force, while on July 1 important provisions of that Bill of Rights were thrown out.

2. On June 30 Legislative Council members were in office for terms scheduled to last until the 1998 elections, while on July 1 they were replaced with a "Provisional Legislature," which was an invention of Beijing, its members approved by Beijing, to rule until the 1998 elections for a new Legislative Council.

3. On June 30 people in Hong Kong who enjoyed freedom of speech could say whatever they wanted, while on July 1 those advocating the independence of Tibet, Taiwan, or Hong Kong were prohibited from advocating those positions.

4. On June 30 any plans for public demonstrations needed only the notification to police so traffic would be stopped for the participants. On July 1 prospective demonstrators of over 50 participants or 30 people in procession had to receive a "no objection" notice from the police seven days in advance. It could be denied for reasons that would be identified at a later time.

5. On June 30 the Tiananmen Square Massacre of 1989 was referred to as "the Tiananmen Square Massacre." On July 1 the Tiananmen Square Massacre was referred to as "the June 4th incident."

All of those preliminary cracks in Hong Kong's foundation were left unsealed. Occasionally there would be an encouraging sign, but they were rare and often superseded by later events. Law Yuk-kai, the director of the Human Rights Monitor in Hong Kong, said, "It is like cooking a frog over a gentle fire. If you raise the temperature little by little, the frog won't know it's being cooked until it's too late."

6. A public announcement was made proclaiming the Provi-

sional Legislature that had been substituted for the then-current Legislative Council was "validly established under Chinese law and was ratified by the [People's Republic of China's] National People's Congress." The provisional body's validity "cannot be challenged by Hong Kong's courts."

7. Hong Kong police were issued guidelines stating they could crack down on demonstrations that "threatened peace" or "backed independence for Tibet or Taiwan." A positive sign was that the annual protests against "the June 4th incident" could continue to take place.

8. Complex election laws for legislators had been initiated by Great Britain and changed by the last British governor of Hong Kong, Chris Patten, to make the Legislative Council progressively more democratic. The laws were then changed by Beijing to slow democracy down. In the elections of 1998, 20 of the 60 legislative seats would be filled by popular vote; 30 seats would be filled by the votes of designated (generally pro-Beijing) business and professional groups; and 10 seats would be determined by an electoral committee of 800 pro-Beijing people.

9. The Provisional Legislature struck down labor laws that had been in effect prior to handover. Many collective bargaining guarantees and protections were stripped away.

1998

10. The Provisional Legislature adopted a document called the "Adaptation of Laws Act." On the surface it seemed to be an unimportant piece of legislation that was simply clarifying some points of law already included in the Basic Law, which was Hong Kong's mini constitution. Under closer examination by democracy advocates, it was discovered that it excluded the new Beijing-approved Hong Kong government and representatives of Beijing's government from laws that would apply to the general public of Hong Kong.

11. A Beijing-appointed committee selected 36 Hong Kong delegates to represent Hong Kong in the parliament of the People's

Republic of China. All the delegates were known to be pro-Beijing.

12. The Hong Kong Journalists Association wrote an official letter to Hong Kong's chief executive, Tung Chee-hwa, complaining that journalists no longer enjoyed the freedom of the press to which they were accustomed under the British.

13. Chief Executive Tung stated that the flag of Taiwan could not be displayed by Hong Kong people as it violates the "one country" principle.

14. Hong Kong film distributors refused to purchase three movies that dealt with the Dalai Lama and Tibet.

15. There was a drenching rain on 1998's election day for the Legislative Council but there were lines of voters waiting outside, bringing about the highest amount of Hong Kong people going to the polls than ever before. Democracy advocates were the overwhelming winners with over 60 percent of the popular vote. But under the formula, democracy advocates ended up with only 17 of the 60 seats of the legislature with 43 seats given to pro-Beijing parties.

16. Human Rights Watch issued a report criticizing the way in which the government "betrayed the principles of democracy" by distorting the election's outcome.

17. When the newly assembled Legislative Council came into session, pro-democracy advocates entered legislation for full direct elections, starting in the year 2002. It was voted down by the pro-Beijing majority.

1999

18. Beijing's National People's Congress overturned an immigration decision made by Hong Kong's Court of Final Appeal. Hong Kong's Court of "Final Appeal" was no longer final.

19. One of the pro-democracy legislators, Margaret Ng, was prohibited from entering the mainland. Other advocates of democ-

racy in Hong Kong were similarly barred from entry into China.

20. Cheng An-kuo, Taiwan's chief representative in Hong Kong, announced on the radio that he agreed with President Lee Teng-hui of Taiwan that any negotiations between Taiwan and the People's Republic of China should be made on a state-to-state basis. He was then told by Beijing and the Hong Kong government that he must refrain from making such comments in Hong Kong even though he was not a citizen of Hong Kong.

21. Beijing announced that Pope John Paul II would not be allowed in Hong Kong on a forthcoming Asian trip since the Vatican maintained diplomatic relations with Taiwan. Hong Kong's chief executive, Tung Chee-hwa, did not protest the decision of Beijing.

22. The Law Reform Commission of the government announced it would establish a Press Council to examine intrusions by the media on privacy rather than have such examinations conducted by any independent group. The council members would be appointed by Chief Executive Tung Chee-hwa.

23. Five U.S. military ships were denied docking rights in Hong Kong's harbor.

24. Chief Executive Tung requested that Szeto Wah abandon any plans for a demonstration to mark the tenth anniversary of the "June 4th incident." Szeto Wah turned him down. The request from the head of Hong Kong's government was perceived by democracy advocates as government pressure that signaled a further departure from the "two systems" guarantee. Due to the courage of Szeto Wah, the demonstration went forward. The government did not issue a further protest.

2000

25. The United States Department of State and the United Kingdom's Foreign Office expressed concern over erosion of freedom of the press in Hong Kong. In response, the Mainland Ministry of For-

eign Affairs emphasized that the "affairs of Hong Kong are Chinese domestic affairs and are not subject to foreign intervention."

26. Beijing discovered that the Internet site, www. hongkong.com had chat rooms in which the independence of Taiwan and Tibet and Hong Kong had been discussed. Those topics were immediately blocked or deleted. The Web site's chairman, Dr. Raymond Chien Kuo-fung, stated that "freedom of speech is not absolute."

27. The People's Republic of China's vice premier, Qian Qichen, said he wanted civil servants in Hong Kong to "better" support Chief Executive Tung. In response to democracy advocates' criticism of Qian Qichen's statement as one of intervention in the Hong Kong's system, Chief Executive Tung answered that Qian's statement was one of "encouragement" only expressing "care" rather than intervention.

28. Hong Kong police arrested university students for participating in an unauthorized assembly protesting the government's planned fees for undergraduate school students.

29. Businesspersons of Hong Kong were warned not to trade with any Taiwanese who advocated Taiwan independence or they would "have to bear all the consequences themselves." They were further redirected to support Chief Executive Tung.

30. The *South China Morning Post* newspaper fired Willy Lam "based on internal restructure." Lam had written about power struggles in Beijing and about the direction given to businesspeople to support Chief Executive Tung.

31. Following Beijing's policies, three Falun Gong practitioners were denied entry into Hong Kong. One was from the United States, one from Japan, and one from Macau.

32. The president of the People's Republic of China, Jiang Zemin, said that Hong Kong and Macau should "function positively in matters concerning the stability and prosperity of Hong Kong and Macau, and the interests of the State and the Chinese Race."

2001

33. A new law of 2001 gave Beijing the ability to remove the chief executive of Hong Kong, rather than having that right rest in Hong Kong's Legislative Council. This new law insured that Beijing would always have the ability to select the leader of its preference rather than the preference of the people of Hong Kong. Martin Lee, the founder and leader of the pro-democracy Democratic Party of Hong Kong, responded, "Tung is happy to be a puppet and he wants to make sure that others who come along will become puppets."

34. Annette Hsiu-lien Lu, the vice president of Taiwan, was a guest on Hong Kong's cable television station. She talked about Taiwan as an independent nation. The Liaison Office of the Central People's Government, under Beijing's direction, said that such talk was prohibited. The Liaison Office released the pronouncement that "Separatist statements should not be treated as ordinary news stories. Hong Kong media has the responsibility to uphold the integrity and sovereignty of the country." In short time it not only became prohibitive to advocate Taiwan's independence, but to even report such advocacy of others.

35. The British House of Commons issued a paper that criticized the mainland government's increasing intervention in Hong Kong's business, violating the promised high degree of autonomy.

36. A delegation of Hong Kong's business executives traveled to Beijing and were told to support Tung Chee-hwa for reelection as chief executive of Hong Kong. Reelection would be performed by the committee of 800. The committee was filled with enough supporters of Beijing to make the selection tantamount to naming the chief executive. It would take 100 members of the committee to nominate a competitor, and that rule meant there would not be a pro-democracy candidate. Tung then announced he would indeed run for a second term, making the announcement one day after the release of a survey in which only 16 percent of Hong Kong people said they supported him for reelection.

37. Jiang Zemin, president of the People's Republic of China,

stated that Hong Kong people enjoyed full freedom. Democracy leader Martin Lee answered, "President Jiang would be right to say we have more freedom—only if he compares Hong Kong with the mainland." Legislator Emily Lau added that: "Hong Kong is going backwards when we compare the political development now with that of the colonial era under former governor Chris Patten...Demonstrations have been under tighter control. Mr. Jiang wants Hong Kong people to feel there is freedom, but it is simply not the truth."

38. The chief of Hong Kong's Civil Service, Anson Chan, a much-respected woman throughout Hong Kong, known as "the conscience of Hong Kong people," resigned from office after being warned by Beijing to give Tung Chee-hwa greater support than they perceived she had given him. She said her decision to resign was for "personal reasons."

39. More than a hundred Falun Gong practitioners were denied visas to Hong Kong. Chief Executive Tung called them "more or less bearing some characteristics of an evil cult." ("Evil cult" was the phrase previously used by the president of the People's Republic of China, Jiang Zemin, to describe the Falun Gong.)

40. The Ministry of Foreign Affairs in Beijing rejected the USS *Inchon*'s port call to Hong Kong.

41. Three travel agencies, Hong Ta Travel Agency, Wing An Travel Agency, and Miramar Travel Agency, were ordered not to call Taipei the capital of Taiwan in any of their brochures.

2002

42. As was preordained, the premier of the People's Republic of China, Zhu Rongji, signed a State Council decree stating that Hong Kong's chief executive Tung Chee-hwa was to start his second five-year term on July 1, 2002. He had garnered the appropriate amount of votes from the 800-member Election Committee (all approved by Beijing). There was no losing candidate (as Tung was the only candidate). After winning reelection, Tung said, "I'm pleased to receive more than seven hundred nominations...I felt that I must win con-

vincingly so people would feel that I am supported by most electors and the community." Audrey Eu of Hong Kong's Legislative Council said the procedure was "a tragedy of our electoral system."

43. The Hong Kong Journalists Association stated that Hong Kong's government had created an environment of self-censorship by the local media regarding issues of which the People's Republic of China's leadership might be sensitive.

44. Beijing refused permission for the USS *Curtis Wilbur* to make a routine port call in Hong Kong.

45. Democracy advocate legislator Emily Lau started a hunger strike outside Central's Star Ferry Terminal to protest Tung's second term.

46. Harry Wu, a Chinese-born American citizen democracy advocate, was refused entry and placed on a flight out of Hong Kong.

47. Demonstrating migrants were dragged out of a Hong Kong park while police tore down their camp.

48. Major democracy advocate and legislator Martin Lee stated, "The changes in Hong Kong have been a slow and steady erosion rather than a single explosion. Rule of law, press freedom, elected institutions, a level economic playing field, and free association have all been battered."

49. The Beijing-appointed government of Hong Kong announced that by July of the coming year, Article 23 of the Basic Law would be put into effect and it would outlaw treason, secession, subversion, sedition, and theft of state secrets. Penalties could range to life imprisonment with the police having the authority to search without warrant. It was unclear what activities would fall under the categories of subversion and sedition.

50. On December 14, an estimated 60,000 people demonstrated in opposition to the government's plan to implement the measures of Article 23.

2003

51. Eighty Taiwanese Falun Gong supporters holding valid visas into Hong Kong who wanted to attend the International Falun Gong Conference were refused entry into Hong Kong and deported.

52. In the face of protests regarding the planned implementation of Article 23, including protest from Catholic Bishop Joseph Zen, the government announced the measures would be revised to be more definitive. Democracy advocates, being suspicious of any definition to come, warned that the entire article should be struck.

53. Regina Ip, the secretary for security who was spearheading the implementation of Article 23, resigned from office for what she claimed were personal reasons.

54. The U.S. House of Representatives passed a resolution introduced by California Congressman Christopher Cox, calling on China to withdraw plans for Article 23 and to allow a democratic legislature in Hong Kong. The resolution passed 426 to 1.

55. On July 1, the sixth anniversary of handover of Hong Kong to the People's Republic of China, more than 500,000 people marched in protest of the pending implementation of Article 23.

56. Censors in Beijing prohibited televised materials, photographs, and stories of the July 1 demonstration and removed such photos from foreign publications before allowing them to be put on sale.

57. Under continuing protests, Tung Chee-hwa indefinitely postponed the implementation of Article 23. Two more of his top officials resigned their offices.

58. The U.S. Commission on International Religious Freedom canceled a visit to China because it prohibited the delegation from visiting Hong Kong. The chairman of the commission, Michael K. Young, said, "It further raises the concern that just six years after the handover, Hong Kong's autonomy is already in serious doubt."

59. In the November 23 local elections, the Democratic Party won 80 percent of the 120 seats it contested while the largest pro-Beijing political party, the Democratic Alliance for the Betterment of Hong Kong (DAB), won only 40 percent of the 206 seats it contested. The DAB's leader, Tsang Yok-sing, said, "It is the worst defeat we have suffered in any of the elections since the DAB was founded eleven years ago."

2004

60. On the first day of January a demonstration attended by an estimated 100,000 people advocated democracy, including universal suffrage to determine the election of the chief executive in 2007 and the entire sixty members of the Legislative Council by 2008. (According to the Basic Law, Hong Kong was supposed to be able to have those rights by 2008.)

61. The New China News Agency published a paper that stated the Government of the People's Republic of China would decide how the next chief executive would be selected as well as the voting requirements for the Legislative Council.

62. Tsang Yok-sing resigned from his party chairmanship of the pro-Beijing DAB political party in the face of the party's defeat of the preceding November.

63. Hong Kong pro-democracy leader and legislator Martin Lee met with U.S. Secretary of State Colin Powell in Washington, D.C., and testified in a U.S. Senate hearing. In reaction, China warned the United States to stop meddling in its internal affairs.

64. In March, vice chairman of the Standing Committee of the National People's Congress in Beijing, Sheng Hua-ren, reaffirmed that Beijing has the authority to declare a state of emergency in Hong Kong and "the Central Government can apply Chinese laws to Hong Kong."

65. China's National People's Congress issued the ruling that full democracy has no timetable. "A locality has no fixed power. All

powers of the locality derive from the authorization of the central authorities."

66. Qiao Xiaoyang of China's National People's Congress stated that "we cannot promise never to interpret the Basic Law in the future." Hong Kong's chief executive Tung Chee-hwa said, "According to the decision there will be no universal suffrage for the chief executive election in 2007, nor will there be for the Legislative Council in 2008...I urge people to stay calm and rational and strive for consensus in the development of Hong Kong."

67. During May three leading radio talk-show hosts resigned. Albert Chang had taken an anti-Beijing view and said he had received death threats, and his trading company was vandalized. That was followed by the resignation of Raymond Wong, who said he was beaten up, had received death threats, and had his noodle shop vandalized. Allen Lee replaced Albert Chang but lasted only two weeks before he resigned. He was a local deputy to China's National People's Congress but came under heavy criticism by the official *China Daily*. Upon resignation, Albert Chang said Beijing forced him to step down. "I cannot express my opinions freely. I don't want to stay in a kitchen with a rising temperature. I just want to get out of the kitchen."

68. The fifteenth anniversary of the Tiananmen Square Massacre drew the largest amount of demonstrators than any of its previous anniversaries since handover. The chairman, Szeto Wah, said, "From the interpretation of the Basic Law to the suppression of universal suffrage and the gags on radio talk-show hosts, I believe everyone in Hong Kong has deep feelings of concern."

69. On July 1, the seventh anniversary of the handover, 530,000 marched for democracy. Yang Wenchang, China's top diplomat in Hong Kong, said, "Hong Kong is our pearl. You can't expect a parent to change his child's future just because he throws a tantrum."

70. Alex Ho, a Hong Kong legislator in the Democratic Party, was arrested in China and was told if he signed a confession that he hired a prostitute, he would be released. If he did not sign the con-

fession he could be prosecuted for rape. After signing, he was not released but sentenced to six months in a labor re-education camp.

71. September elections for the Legislative Council gave pro-democracy parties a gain of three additional seats but that was a disappointment to them, as it was expected they would gain a good deal more. The leading democracy party, the Democratic Party, lost two of its eleven seats it had held. This time, half of the Legislative Council was elected by popular vote and the other half by proportional representation; professional and industrial and business groups called functional constituencies, which were mainly business and pro-Beijing advocates. In total, democracy activists won 62 percent of the votes, but awarded only 40 percent of the legislative seats. Pro-Beijing candidates took 37 percent of the votes but were given 60 percent of the seats.

72. At the celebration of the fifth anniversary (December 20) of Macau's handover to China, president of the People's Republic of China Hu Jintao praised Macau in successfully implementing "one country, two systems" and that political power must be kept in the hands of "patriots" loyal to China in both Macau and Hong Kong. At that ceremony, in which Hong Kong's chief executive Tung Chee-hwa was present, Hu turned to Tung and told him to "look for inadequacies" and to "continue to raise the quality of governing." This was widely perceived as a public dressing-down of Tung Chee-hwa in view of Hong Kong people's demonstrations for democracy.

2005

73. On January 21 an estimated 8,000 Hong Kong people demonstrated for full democracy, many wearing black ribbons in memory of Zhao Ziyang of China who died a week earlier in Beijing. (Zhao had sympathized with demonstrators in Tiananmen Square and spent the last fifteen years of his life under house arrest.) They chanted, "Mourn Ziyang!" and "Release democracy campaigners!" Banners read, "End One-Party Rule!"

74. Pro-democracy members of the Legislative Council observed one minute of silence for Zhao Ziyang. The Legislative Council's

president, Rita Fan, rejected their request for the entire legislature to honor Zhao.

75. A poll taken by the Hong Kong University Public Opinion Program asked, "If a general election of the chief executive was to be held tomorrow, and you had the right to vote, would you vote for Tung Chee-hwa?" "Yes" received 18.1 percent, "No" received 65.5 percent, and "Not Sure" received 16.5 percent

76. Chief Executive Tung Chee-Hwa was appointed vice chairman of Beijing's Chinese People's Political Consultative Conference (CPPCC), a position he held prior to becoming chief executive of Hong Kong, and a position traditionally offered to retired officials. This was perceived as a step toward being told to leave his current position by Beijing, whose government believed his lack of popularity led to the rise and encouragement of the pro-democracy movement of Hong Kong.

77. Tung Chee-hwa announced his resignation as chief executive on March 10. "An hour ago I tendered my resignation as chief executive...My health is not as good as it used to be. If I continue as chief executive, I won't be able to handle it." His chief secretary, Donald Tsang (Yam Kuen), was named as acting (interim) chief executive until a new one was to be named in four months on July 10 by the selection committee of 800. It was certain Donald Tsang would be their choice. Anyone wanting to run against him as a nominee was still under the rule that called for a minimum of 100 votes for nomination of the committee of 800, and the committee of 800 was "in the pocket" of Beijing not only for the winner but for any nominee. The major unknown was if the selected chief executive would fill only the remaining two years of Tung Chee-hwa's term or be given a full five-year term. Hong Kong's democracy advocates believed Hong Kong should make that decision and not Beijing.

78. Acting Chief Executive Donald Tsang gave a statement at a news conference that Taiwan should follow Hong Kong's example and become unified with the People's Republic of China under the "one country, two systems" formula. He said Hong Kong would "spare no effort" to help unify Taiwan with China. "We believe

we have demonstrated that a capitalist system in Hong Kong is operating very successfully within the framework of the Chinese nation." Foreign correspondents asked Donald Tsang when democracy of "one man, one vote" would come to Hong Kong, and asked Tsang's view of democracy. Tsang answered, "My vision is irrelevant in this...When you say 'one man, one vote' in our legislature, we have to define exactly what that is." (Tsang had served thirty-eight years working for the British government and had even been knighted by Prince Charles.)

79. Beijing made the decision that the next chief executive (certain to be Donald Tsang) would serve an interim two-year term rather than a five-year term. That contingency was not addressed in the Basic Law. Fifteen hundred citizens demonstrated against the decision being made by Beijing rather than Hong Kong. The demonstration was not directed against Donald Tsang, whose popularity was far above that of the former chief executive, Tung Chee-hwa, but Hong Kong democracy advocates believed "one country, two systems" was "becoming more and more of a hoax" and that the two-year term was wanted by Beijing as a probationary period to judge Donald Tsang's loyalty to Beijing.

80. Hong Kong operations of the daily newspaper the *Epoch Times* were forced to stop printing. An open letter from the *Epoch Times* stated, "Due to fear of people learning the truth, the Chinese Communist Party has exerted hard and soft pressure on the printing house that prints the *Epoch Times*." The *Epoch Times* had openly reported on Tibet, human rights, Falun Gong, the AIDS epidemic in China, and was the first media to break the story on SARS.

81. Ching Cheong, a Hong Kong–based reporter for Singapore's *Straits Times* was detained in China for allegedly obtaining state secrets.

82. The Committee to Protect Journalists ranked the People's Republic of China as the foremost government imprisoning journalists.

83. The annual demonstration in Hong Kong's Victoria Park to commemorate the anniversary of the Tiananmen Square Massacre

drew 45,000 demonstrators raising candles and carrying signs that read, "Don't forget June 4" and "Democracy Fighters Live Forever." Earlier that day Donald Tsang, representing the government, said, "I had shared Hong Kong people's passion and impetus when the June 4 incident happened. But after sixteen years, I've seen our country's impressive economic and social development. My feelings have become calmer." In China, where an estimated 250 survivors of the massacre were still imprisoned, the government imposed tightened security at Tiananmen Square with extra carloads of police to prevent any commemoration. Relatives of those who had lost their lives there, once again had their residences encircled by police. There was no public mention of the anniversary in Beijing.

84. Without denials by officials of the Yahoo Internet firm, it was reported that Yahoo, which was registered in Hong Kong, provided information regarding a journalist, Shi Tao, to Chinese officials, who then accused Shi Tao of e-mailing "state secrets" and sentenced him to ten years imprisonment. Yahoo's response was, "Yahoo must ensure that its local country sites must cooperate within the laws, regulations, and customs." (Unlike democracies, state secrets of the PRC go well beyond national security, including information on statistics, child labor laws, police behavior, strikes, riots, and other government data. Moreover, the answer of Yahoo put into further question Hong Kong's autonomy guaranteed under "one country, two systems.") Reporters Without Borders accused Yahoo–Hong Kong of helping China's government to trace the e-mails of Shi Tao. Court documents confirmed Yahoo Holdings Ltd. in Hong Kong worked with the PRC government to find Shi Tao. (Reportedly, he had e-mailed personal notes on media restrictions from a staff meeting while working for the financial publication *Contemporary Business News*.) Lo King-wah, spokesman for the Hong Kong Journalists Association, condemned Shi Tao's sentencing, stating that Shi Tao did not expose a state secret and that the help given to the PRC by Yahoo–Hong Kong was detrimental to press freedom. When asked if Yahoo gave the PRC Shi Tao's address, Pauline Wong, spokesperson of Yahoo–Hong Kong, responded she was "unable to give out information like that."

85. Donald Tsang became the "elected" chief executive. Two

people had tried to run against him but failed to get a nomination since they did not receive the 100 votes required of the election committee of 800.

86. A woman from Hong Kong visiting China was dragged to a hospital in an attempt to force her to abort a six-month-old fetus under the government's one-child policy. Her relatives stopped them, contacted Hong Kong authorities, and she was freed without an abortion.

87. China formally charged Ching Cheong, the Hong Kong journalist working for the Singapore newspaper, the *Straits Times*, of spying for Taiwan. He had been arrested (previously mentioned) in April of 2005.

88. All 60 members of the Hong Kong Legislative Council were invited to Guangdong, PRC, for a two-day visit for an "honest dialogue." Lee Cheuk-san, democracy advocate from the Legislative Council, asked Provisional Party Chief Zhang Dejiang for the government to reappraise the official position on the Tiananmen Square Massacre. Zhang answered that only a minority of people supported "redressing June 4" and that the party had handled the "incident" correctly. When some in the Hong Kong delegation objected to the answer, Zhang Dejiang responded that the conversation had become disagreeable and that any further discussion would be a "waste of breath."

89. After democracy advocates demanded universal suffrage, Hong Kong's chief executive, Donald Tsang, proposed expanding the Legislative Council from 60 members to 70 members, with five of the new ten to be elected by the people in general elections and the other five to be selected by the city's 529 district councilors. (The chief executive appoints 102 of those district councilors. Governor Chris Patten, the last governor under British rule, had abolished appointed district seats, but they were restored after Hong Kong was handed over to the PRC.) Donald Tsang also proposed the number of people voting for chief executive should be expanded from 800 to 1,600. The democracy advocates of the Legislative Council opposed the offers since they said the proposals were "a

sham" and "less than a bone" to the people of Hong Kong, who want universal suffrage, and the guarantees of Hong Kong's management of its internal affairs under "one country, two systems."

90. Among 153 new non-official members of Chief Executive Donald Tsang's Commission on Strategic Development were seven members of the Democratic Party. The commission's purpose is to advise the chief executive on policy matters including universal suffrage, for the chief executive's acceptance or rejection.

91. Once again, democracy-advocate Martin Lee went to Washington, D.C., where he met with U.S. Secretary of State Condoleezza Rice. Her spokesperson said, "The secretary emphasized our conviction that the people of Hong Kong should determine the pace and scope of political reform in accordance with the Basic Law. We support democracy and universal suffrage in Hong Kong."

92. On December 4, an estimated 250,000 demonstrated in Hong Kong in support of universal suffrage. Catholic Bishop Joseph Zen gave the benediction at Victoria Park. Mock bird cages had been placed near the podium to symbolize the imprisonment of democracy. An announcement that former chief secretary Anson Chan (known as "the Conscience of Hong Kong") had joined the demonstrators brought about a crowd-wide ovation.

93. That evening Chief Executive Donald Tsang told a news conference that "I have heard their voice, I have felt their feelings and I share their pursuit, and the central government [of Hong Kong] perfectly understands their aspirations." He added that he has "little scope." That was interpreted to be an obvious reference to the authority of the People's Republic of China.

94. In response to the December demonstration of Hong Kong people, the deputy spokesman for the U.S. State Department, Adam Ereli, said, "We believe it's important to achieve universal suffrage in Hong Kong as soon as possible, that the people of Hong Kong are ready for democracy, and that the sooner that a timetable for achieving universal suffrage is established, the better. And it's certainly, I think, the spirit in which the demonstrations took place."

Spokesman for the Foreign Ministry of the People's Republic of China, Qin Gang, responded to the United States by saying: "Hong Kong affairs are China's domestic affairs, and do not allow for any foreign intervention. The U.S. side has repeatedly made indiscreet comments on the affairs of the Hong Kong Special Administrative Region, which is very inappropriate and we are in firm opposition to such comments."

2006

95. Hong Kong's Bishop Joseph Zen, a staunch critic of the People's Republic of China's infringement of religious freedom, was chosen to be a cardinal by Pope Benedict XVI. Liu Bainan, the vice president of China's State Catholic Patriotic Association, which does not recognize the pope (controlling China's "state-sanctioned only" Catholic churches), said it was a "hostile act" and the pope showed a lack of respect for China by choosing Bishop Zen without prior consultation with the Beijing's leadership. On Hong Kong Radio he said, "Why would you appoint someone who doesn't support communism as a cardinal? Is it like Poland? Didn't the church play a big role in Poland?…If China's bishops were all like him then it would be dangerous like Poland. Bishop Zen is widely known as an opponent of communism." China's Foreign Ministry spokesman, Liu Jianchao, issued a statement: "We have taken note of Zen's appointment. We advocate that religious figures should not interfere with politics." The underground communications (or as it is called, the "Small Lane News") in China had long passed the rumor that when Pope John Paul II appointed new cardinals in 2003, that he kept secret the name of one of those appointed, and he was Chinese. Now the rumor was that it was Hong Kong's Joseph Zen.

96. There was a break-in of the Hong Kong office of the *Epoch Times*, smashing the glass entrance door with sledge hammers. Four men then entered the computer room and smashed a $129,000 computer component that transferred electronic layout files to press-ready metal plates. They threatened to beat the employees if they called the police. The *Epoch Times* was known as a critic of Beijing's policies and had recently printed a widely distributed book of the crimes of that government.

97. Democracy advocates of Hong Kong requested that Hong Kong's people be allowed to vote for their own delegates within Beijing's National People's Congress instead of the policy of Hong Kong's representatives being appointed by the Chinese Communist Party (with the Hong Kong delegation including those who did not live in Hong Kong). The response from Jiang Enzhu, spokesman for Beijing's National People's Congress, was that "there is no plan to change the current method for electing deputies to the National People's Congress."

98. Hong Kong's *South China Morning Post* printed a summary of the decline in Hong Kong's expatriate population. The British were down 24 percent, Canadians down 18 percent, Australians down 15 percent, and Americans down 5 percent.

99. British expatriates in Hong Kong were banned from singing their national anthem at a cathedral service celebrating the Queen's eightieth birthday.

100. Legislators and democracy advocates Martin Lee, Albert Chang, and Leung Kwok-hung publicly charged that their phones had been tapped. The allegations were not confirmed or denied but the secretary for security said the government had not done anything illegal.

101. A new pro-democracy political party, the Civic Party was inaugurated. All Hong Kong political parties are allowed to keep their membership confidential but, according to the *South China Morning Post*, the Central Government's Hong Kong office had been asking professionals and businesspeople about their affiliation with the new party.

102. The People's Republic of China "ordained" Ma Yinglin and Liu Xinhong to be bishops without the approval of the Vatican. A spokesman for Pope Benedict XVI said the pope had expressed profound displeasure. The Vatican called the act of the People's Republic of China a violation of religious freedom and excommunicated Ma Yinglin and Liu Xinhong.

103. On April 27, the Beijing government held a public meeting of legal scholars in which deputy dean of Tsinghua's University's Law School, Wang Zhenmin, said in his opinion Hong Kong could be granted democracy on a set of conditions including Hong Kong's legislature passing national security legislation (the kind that was protested in 2003) and if Hong Kong would have a greater emphasis on "patriotic education." Another scholar, Xu Chongde, added that such democracy would call for Hong Kong people electing a leader who was "a patriot."

104. Quincy Jones was hired to organize a music festival for the year 2007 to celebrate the tenth anniversary of Hong Kong's handover from Great Britain to the People's Republic of China. Jones was quoted by *Deutsche Press-Agentur* as saying, "We are planning to make the festival part of a series of events across the mainland, like Shanghai and Beijing."

105. The annual commemoration remembering the Tiananmen Square Massacre took place the night of June 4 in Hong Kong's Victoria Park with an estimated 44,000 participants, most holding lit candles. They sang the song "Freedom Flower" with the lyrics, "No matter how heavy the rain beats, freedom will blossom."

106. Anson Chan (as stated earlier, she had been the former chief secretary of Tung Chee-hwa, and was widely known as "the Conscience of Hong Kong") announced she would take part in the Saturday, July 1, rally for democracy, the same day as the ninth anniversary of the handover of Hong Kong to the People's Republic of China. Anson Chan, in announcing her intention to participate in the democracy rally, said, "I want to stress that this is not my personal show. Democracy belongs to all." She urged Hong Kong people to attend the rally.

107. This was followed by a surprising announcement from Regina Ip, the former secretary for security under Tung Chee-hwa. She was known as a hardliner for Beijing mandates, often called "Red Regina" by democracy advocates, and she was the chief supporter and front-person for the infamous Article 23 Anti-Subversion Bill. She often spoke against holding free elections by universal suffrage.

In June of 2003 she resigned in the wake of massive demonstrations against Article 23 and went to the United States for three years. She made a return to Hong Kong in June 2006, and within days of her return announced that she has sided with democracy advocates, stating, "The only way forward is complete democratization."

108. The Hong Kong government announced the program for the handover's ninth anniversary celebrations, including a ceremony at eight in the morning with Chief Executive David Tsang in Wan Chai with 2,500 guests and 1,000 members of the public at large. "The square and its vicinity will be designated a restricted zone by police to ensure smooth running of the ceremony. Only holders of valid passes can enter."

109. On Saturday, July 1, separate and apart from the government celebration of the Handover Anniversary Celebration, the day started with a prayer meeting in Victoria Park attended by Cardinal Joseph Zen. He requested that Hong Kong people "persist in fighting for early universal suffrage." The chairman of Hong Kong's Catholic Diocese's Justice and Peace, Lisa Leung Yuk-ming, added, "The government has been making excuses to deprive us of our political rights." Then came the pro-democracy rally titled "Strive for Full Democracy" with banners stating, "Justice, Equality, Fight for Democracy." (Police estimated 28,000 attended, while the organizers estimated the number at 58,000. The government's parade celebrating the anniversary of handover was estimated by both organizers and police as attended by 40,000.) A ring of people at the pro-democracy rally held hands providing a security circle around Anson Chan. One participant at the pro-democracy rally, Au Kit-lin, said, "It's precisely because Beijing rejected our demands that I have to come out and shout so they'll know what we want." Wang Bei said, "The society is far from harmonious now. I must treasure my right to protest and fight for full voting rights." Two of the most important Hong Kong figures gave statements of great contrast: at the government's official rally to celebrate handover, Chief Executive David Tsang focused on the economy, stating, "As our economy gains momentum in its growth, we must grasp the opportunity to keep it in good shape so that we could live up to our country's expectations for Hong Kong." Away from that celebration, at

the prayer meeting of mainly Catholic democracy advocates in Victoria Park, Cardinal Zen focused on liberty, stating, "This is the ninth anniversary of the establishment of the Hong Kong Special Administrative Region. The Basic Law promised the people of Hong Kong a high degree of autonomy but the present situation seems to contradict this affirmation. There has been no progress, and in fact it seems that there have been some setbacks."

To the detriment of Hong Kong and to the benefit of Taiwan, an example of "one country, two systems" has been established. Since the 1997 handover, Hong Kong has progressively become less and less unique. Not visually. To the tourist, the businessperson, and most travelers, the changes in Hong Kong are not obvious. The skyline remains spectacular, the hotels are still luxurious, the streets are as crowded as ever, and the shopping centers are unmanageably chaotic. The visuals are still magnificent, while most visitors have no way to know the chronology of the invisible. Anson Chan had warned that Hong Kong could become "just another Chinese city."

Not yet.

Since Beijing has offered its "one country, two systems" arrangement to Taiwan, it is entirely possible that Beijing will be sure that its domination over Hong Kong will not be readily apparent to the international visitor until China achieves its planned jurisdiction over Taiwan. If that day should come, the "one country, two systems" promise to Hong Kong, Macau, and to Taiwan will be known as a takeover rather than a handover.

Knowing what we have seen in the years since handover, "one country, two systems" has become, as predicted by Law Yuk-kai, the "frog over a gentle fire," with the temperature rising. And there is the unanswered question: Why was there a time limit specified for the "one country, two systems" status of Hong Kong? What is supposed to happen in the termination year of 2047?

No need to dwell on it. It's happening earlier.

Chapter Twelve

EMBASSIES FOR SALE

A T THIS WRITING only twenty-four nations are left that have diplomatic relations with Taiwan; the more recent conversions from Taiwan to the People's Republic of China having been made for a reward of millions of dollars in obvious offers of bribery by the PRC. Taiwan has been accused of doing the same thing. If true, Taiwan has been doing a crummy job.

It used to be that dollar diplomacy was only talked about privately. It was publicly exposed when Jason Hu, Taiwan's foreign minister, said that the Central African Republic broke off relations with Taiwan after Taiwan refused to give the Central African Republic a $120 million loan, and that the Central African Republic had a history of threatening the switching of diplomatic relations between Taipei and Beijing.

In another example, Jason Hu said that Guinea-Bissau requested "a huge amount of financial aid" to retain diplomatic relations.

Recently such extortion has become more frequent and even publicly admitted:

Diplomatic relations with the Caribbean island nation of Dominica were bought by Beijing in 2004 for a promised $117 million.

The South Pacific island nation of Vanuatu was bought in 2004 with the prime minister of Vanuatu, Serge Vohor, defending his decision by saying, "We want to work with China and Taiwan together in our country in the Melanesian spirit of solidarity. Their fight has nothing to do with us and we want to be friends with both countries because we need the money." At least he didn't kid around. Being friends with both, of course, meant breaking diplomatic relations with Taiwan, since the People's Republic of China makes that a condition for diplomatic recognition, while Taiwan never insists on a nation breaking relations with the People's Republic of China so as to have them with Taiwan.

Perhaps most surprising and worst of all was the January 2005 decision of Grenada, a nation that had been liberated from a communist coup in 1983 by the United States. The gratitude of Grenada's people was well-known throughout the world. As much as Grenada wanted freedom, that nation's later leader, Prime Minister Keith Mitchell, did not seem to have the same attitude toward others. Taiwan was Grenada's largest aid donor when there was no threat of losing diplomatic relations to Beijing. After Hurricane Ivan in mid-2004, Taiwan gave an immediate $4.7 million package with a promise to give $40 million so Grenada could rebuild a devastated sports stadium prior to the 2007 Cricket World Cup event to be hosted by Grenada.

Not enough.

Suddenly there came the unexpected threat of switching diplomatic relations. In order to retain diplomatic relations with Taiwan, Grenada prime minister Keith Mitchell was clear. Such retention would call for a massive financial package, including paying off Grenada's national debt. When that was rejected, Prime Minister Mitchell went on a trip to Beijing. Within weeks from Prime Minister Mitchell's return home, Grenada announced the establishment of diplomatic relations with the People's Republic of China.

Taiwan's embassy staff packed their bags.

In May of 2005, Taiwan's President Chen was visiting South Pacific nations and had a stopover in Fiji, a nation having diplomatic relations with the People's Republic of China. During the stopover President Chen was met by the vice president of Fiji and some other officials of Fiji. The People's Republic of China was immediate in issuing an angry statement blaming Fiji's government for breaching bilateral commitments that endorsed the adoption of a "one China" policy by allowing President Chen to land there.

One week later there was a bright note in what was the surprise reestablishment of diplomatic recognition with Taiwan by President Ludwig Scotty of the West Central Pacific nation of Nauru. The previous president, Rene Harris, had switched diplomatic relations from Taiwan to the People's Republic of China. Ludwig Scotty, now having attained the office of the president, and having visited Taiwan earlier to attend a conference on democracy and freedom, switched back to Taiwan, giving up diplomatic relations with the People's Republic of China.

The day after that, Taiwan's premier, Frank Hsieh, was barred from visiting Germany and Austria, as China had told those two governments not to issue visas to Frank Hsieh. He wanted to travel there to visit Siemens AG, the electrical engineering and electronics company that was the main contractor in rapid transit and light rail systems in Kaohsiung, Taiwan. An invitation from Siemens was made earlier while Premier Hsieh was mayor of Kaohsiung. Siemens tried to persuade both Germany and Austria to allow Premier Hsieh's visit but to no avail, since China prohibited those nations from having any formal contact with Taiwan officials.

In August of 2006, the African nation of Chad traded in diplomatic relations from Taiwan to the People's Republic of China. That caused leaders in Taiwan's government to travel to several allied nations for meetings with their leaders in the hope of preventing further erosion of relations.

Most nations of the world, including democracies—even including the United States—treat elected officials of Taiwan as pariahs who look through our windows, but can't come in.

In all of Europe there was only country that retained diplomatic relations with Taiwan. And it had nothing at all to do with dollar diplomacy. It was a very small country in territory but a very large one in importance. The country was the Holy See.

CHAPTER THIRTEEN

POPE JOHN PAUL II, CHINA, AND TAIWAN

THE TOP NEWS STORY of the day in the press of the People's Republic of China concerned a tree-planting campaign. They certainly had an exclusive since the day's top story in most countries of the world was that Pope John Paul II died.

The Vatican and the People's Republic of China had severed relations in 1951 with Beijing demanding the Vatican break diplomatic relations with Taiwan and warning the Vatican "not to interfere in China's internal affairs" regarding Taiwan and religious affairs. "Interference in religious affairs" stems from the PRC policy that all Catholic groups in China are required to register with the "Catholic Patriotic Association." That group appoints bishops and does not recognize those appointed by the Vatican.

Adding to the discord between the Vatican and the Beijing government was that just prior to the Tiananmen Square Massacre in 1989 the pope had made clear and definitive statements that the voices of the demonstrators in Tiananmen Square should be heard.

Two years after the handover of Hong Kong from Great Britain to the People's Republic of China, Beijing ordered that Pope John Paul II could not enter Hong Kong during a forthcoming Asian trip.

There's more. The People's Republic of China's government placed an unaccepted demand that the pope withdraw the October 1, 2000, canonization of 120 Catholic missionaries, both foreign and Chinese, who became martyrs when they were murdered in China between the years 1648 and 1930. All of that happened long before the communist government took over, but the communist government states that the missionaries "were executed for violation of Chinese laws during the invasion of China by imperialists and colonialists."

Pope John Paul II had made many attempts to have relations with Beijing and a joining of the Beijing recognized Catholic Church with the underground Catholic Church, but the conditions of the People's Republic of China did not change, and the pope would not accept their conditions.

When the pope died in 2005 the PRC's foreign ministry spokesman, Liu Jianchao, issued a statement that "we express condolences for the passing of Pope John Paul II. We hope that under the leadership of a new pope, favorable conditions for improving China-Vatican relations can be made."

The "Catholic Patriotic Association" issued a statement of "deep sorrow on the part of China's four million [registered] Catholics" and requested them to pray for the pope and hold memorial services and expressed their wish that "the successor to Pope John Paul II would pursue the unfinished task of normalizing ties with Beijing." In the headquarters of that association at South Cathedral in Beijing, Father Peter Zhao Jianmin said, "We hope the dear old man prays for us in heaven."

They still wanted something from him.

The underground Catholic Church, with an estimated eight to twelve million followers, expressed their grief over the death of the pope through word of mouth in "Small Lane News." "It is a very sad moment and everyone's hearts are heavy" was a statement made by an officer of the underground Catholic Church. The officer's name was held in anonymity, as known authorities and leaders are arrested and even the names of members are held in secrecy since members can also be arrested and, if not arrested, are routinely harassed and denied social services.

Father Louis Shen, a priest in Taipei, was taken prisoner in Shanghai in 1958 when he was twenty-two years old. As an admitted follower of Roman Catholicism, he was accused of counterrevolutionary conduct. He was sentenced to three years in prison followed by twenty-five years of hard labor. He was released in late 1985 and given Chinese currency worth approximately a hundred U.S. dollars in compensation for the time he served. He said: "The idea was reform through labor, so we had to endure two main hardships: not having enough to eat and physical exhaustion. We had to go outdoors in sub-zero temperatures and they would shout, 'Work hard! If you work hard, you won't freeze to death.' People who protested were beaten or chained."

A Vatican-appointed bishop, Kung Pin-Mei, later appointed as Cardinal Kung, was also arrested by the PRC and imprisoned for thirty-three years.

Hours after the death of Pope John Paul II, Beijing announced that Chinese authorities had carried out a new series of arrests of officials from the underground church.

Qin Gang, a spokesman for the Foreign Ministry said that China "is ready to improve relations with the Vatican" but then came the old cry, "provided it severs diplomatic recognition with Taiwan and that it does not interfere in the internal affairs of China in the name of religion." Meaning, of course, that the atheist government of Beijing must appoint Catholic bishops in China and the pope could not.

Pope John Paul II had yet to be entombed and a new pope had yet to be named by the College of Cardinals when rumors in Hong Kong and Taiwan circulated that "foreign officials" were telling them that with a new pope, the Vatican might give up Taiwan for diplomatic relations with the People's Republic of China. No one revealed where the rumors originated but it is certainly possible that any number of foreign nations could have had foreign service officers with political advocacies who advertised them as soon as Pope John Paul II was gone.

In Taiwan, where flags flew at half-staff over government buildings, President Chen Shui-bian said, "The world has lost a great religious leader...He will always be remembered for his lifelong efforts to seek peace and happiness for all mankind." The president mentioned the reception the pope gave for President Chen's wife, First Lady Wu Shu-jen, in 2003 and that the pope gave her a rosary. "It was a touching moment for all Taiwanese people to remember when the two shook hands from their wheelchairs," President Chen said. The president added that he would always abide "by the pope's four pillars of peace: truth, justice, love, and freedom."

The Vatican invited President Chen to attend the funeral of Pope John Paul II. He accepted the invitation.

There had never been an official trip to Europe by any president of Taiwan. In 2001 President Chen was awarded the 2001 Freedom Award from a European-based human rights organization for his contributions to democratization and his "solid record as a human rights activist." The award was to be presented in Copenhagen but Denmark would not issue him a visa. The group decided to present the award in Strasbourg, but France, too, refused him a visa. The only way it could be presented was for President Chen's wife, Wu Shu-jen, to go to France on an unofficial tourist-style trip and pick up the award for her husband.

President Chen's decision to attend Pope John Paul II's funeral was followed immediately with the announcement from Beijing that in response to Chen's attendance there would be no attendance from anyone from the People's Republic of China.

There was another issue. Since the Vatican had no airport, those flying to a Vatican ceremony would land in Italy. Beijing tried to pressure Italy not to allow President Chen to land. Italy disregarded Beijing's demand. President Chen's office issued a statement that "President Chen expresses gratitude for the Vatican's invitation as well as to the Italian government for granting him the visa." He would stay overnight at the Excelsior Hotel in Rome.

Beijing spokesman Qin Gang reacted by saying, "His real intention is to take this opportunity to engage in secessionist activity and create two Chinas or one China and one Taiwan, which is what we are opposed to." The deputy head of China's State Chinese Catholic Patriotic Association, Liu Bainian, repeated that the PRC would not send any representative and that "the decision to let Chen Shui-bian attend has hurt the feelings of the Chinese people, including five million Catholics."

The funeral was blacked out of China's state-controlled media, its audience left with a two-sentence report stating that it had taken place. There were no other reports or pictures in its newspapers or on television. CNN was blacked out every time the funeral was reported. China's top Internet service providers removed discussions of the pope, saying they feared that non-believers would be disrespectful to Catholics.

President Chen was hailed back at home and in much of Europe, where his invitation and attendance was called a "diplomatic coup."

Coincidentally, at the same time as President Chen's trip, the Dalai Lama arrived in Tokyo where he paid tribute to Pope John Paul II, with whom he had repeatedly met. The Chinese Foreign Ministry issued a statement: "We strongly demand Japan to take pragmatic steps to honor its solemn promise on the Tibet issue to prevent the Dalai Lama from visiting Japan and not to provide a stage for his political activities."

After Pope John Paul II was entombed and the College of Cardinals elected Joseph Ratzinger as the new pope, becoming Benedict XVI, Beijing's Foreign Ministry spokesman Qin Gang (unsurprisingly) stated: "We are willing to improve the relationship between China and the Vatican on the basis of two principles. One is that Joseph Ratzinger should break off the so-called diplomatic relationship with Taiwan and recognize that the government of the People's Republic of China is the only legitimate government which represents China, and that Taiwan is an inseparable part of China. The second is that Ratzinger should not interfere in internal Chinese affairs, including in the name of religion. We hope that with a new pope, the Vatican can create conditions to improve China-Vatican relations."

While the Vatican received visitors from around the world, the People's Republic of China greeted a visitor of its own: Prime Minister Jean-Pierre Raffarin of France.

CHAPTER FOURTEEN

BON AMI CHINA, *AU REVOIR* TAIWAN, *TOMODACHI* TAIWAN, *SAYONARA* CHINA

T HE "ANTI-SECESSION LAW," France's prime minister Jean-Pierre Raffarin said, "is completely compatible with the position of France." He was in Beijing on April 21, 2005, at a press conference standing next to Wen Jiabo, the premier of the People's Republic of China. Prime Minister Jean-Pierre Raffarin continued his statement by supporting the lifting of the European embargo of arms and technology to the People's Republic of China, calling the fifteen-year embargo that started in retaliation for the Tiananmen Square Massacre "anachronistic, wrongfully discriminatory, and in complete contradiction of the current state of the strategic partnership between Europe and China." He went on to say, "France believes that the transition in progress will leave China even stronger and a responsible great nation respected and at peace with neighbors, a new focus of stability on the international scene...France continues to require the lifting of the embargo and does not see what could lead the European Council to change its position on the subject."

Not coincidentally, Prime Minister Raffarin's visit did not end until he finalized business agreements with Beijing valued at approximately $3.2 billion. Airplane deals alone with the Toulouse-based Airbus totaled between $500 and $600 million from Chinese airlines. "This is a very big market," Philippe Delmas, vice president of Airbus, said (who accompanied Prime Minister Raffarin to Beijing). "In the first four months of the year it grew 40 percent over the same period last year."

China's People's Liberation Army was intending to purchase 210 Mirage 2000-9CS fighters, far superior to the 60 2000-5E's purchased in the mid-1990s by Taiwan. Chinese pilots arrived in France for training on the new advanced fighter aircraft.

While France was embracing China, China was engaged in sudden unprecedented demonstrations against Japan. The public issue charged by China was that eight schoolbooks in Japan glossed over Japanese Empire atrocities committed against the Chinese in World War II. "It is not China that bears the blame for letting Sino-Japanese relations come to this pass," the PRC's Foreign Ministry spokesman, Qin Gang, said. "Japan must conscientiously and appropriately deal with its history of invading China."

Thousands of Chinese demonstrated against Japan throughout Beijing, Shanghai, Xiamen, Shengyang, Chengdu, Guangzhou, and Shenzhen, smashing windows of Japanese enterprises with bricks, stones, and bottles. The PRC's government denied it authorized the demonstrations but the denial was not taken seriously since the expertise of the police in breaking up demonstrations was internationally known. In this case, police turned their backs on the demonstrations even when the Japanese Embassy in Beijing and the Japanese Consulate in Shanghai were attacked and damaged by demonstrators. Police also ignored the same treatment given by demonstrators to other official missions of Japan and to Japanese enterprises. Stores, shops, and restaurants were battered and Japanese students were attacked. No one was arrested. There were, instead, signs posted that indicated to the demonstrators the directions of the march.

The Japanese government answered that the schoolbooks in Japan that glossed over Japanese Empire atrocities committed against the Chinese in World War II were written and released by private companies, not the government, and those books had only a small release to a few schools. The government added that it had apologized some seventeen times for atrocities committed in China during World War II, as well as having given billions of dollars in aid to China. Japan's prime minister Koizumi then added to the list of Japan's admissions of atrocities "with feelings of deep remorse and heartfelt apology…In the past, Japan, through its colonial rule and aggression, caused tremendous damage and suffering for the people of many countries, particularly those of Asian nations. Japan squarely faces these facts of history in a spirit of humility."

Japan's foreign minister, Nobutaka Machimura, was not quite as defensive. He said, "From the perspective of a Japanese person, *Chinese* textbooks appear to teach that everything the Chinese government has done has been correct. There is a tendency towards this in any country, but the Chinese textbooks are extreme in the way they uniformly convey the 'our country is correct' perspective." He then said Japan's government would make a full review of Chinese textbooks and officially inform Beijing of the results of their review.

After three weekends of massive and destructive demonstrations, the government of the People's Republic of China called for citizens not to take part in the anti-Japan protests as they could affect social stability. That was all that was needed. The demonstrations stopped.

Those sudden public exhibitions against Japan in cities of China may have been spontaneous and they may have taken place without government approval, and they may have had everything to do with the textbooks in Japan. But the chronology of events at least raised suspicions that they might have had something to do with government anger over the recent U.S.-Japan Joint Agreement stating that security in the Taiwan Strait "is a common strategic objective."

CHAPTER FIFTEEN

THE IMPORTANCE OF LANGUAGE TRAINING

B EFORE U.S. FOREIGN SERVICE OFFICERS leave to go to a new post overseas, they often go to a language training school for a quick course in the language of their assigned host country. They don't come out of that school being able to speak fluently in the language they quickly study, but at least they know the essentials.

Long before they ever get there, however, they become fluent in the language of the State Department or they would never get an overseas assignment. Learning that language is not as easy as mastering a foreign tongue because it requires the placement of English words into sentences that sound informative but do not inform.

A prime example has been in use since the meetings of President Eisenhower with foreign leaders, all the way to President George W. Bush with foreign leaders. State Department foreign service officers describing such meetings to the press have learned to say, "It was a useful and constructive meeting in which a wide range of subjects were discussed." It doesn't mean anything, and the meeting might not have been useful at all, as well as being unconstructive while only one subject was discussed.

The U.S. State Department teaches creative use of ambiguity particularly when discussing a conflict between two foreign nations if there is no question that one side is to blame and the other side is guiltless. With few exceptions, the language demands that in such a case, equal responsibility should be given to both parties to the conflict.

When it is simply beyond any pretense that a foreign government has done something absolutely outrageous, the skilled language-master must choose to say the foreign nation's action is "unhelpful." That shows thoughtfulness rather than emotion. And it is important to go easy on the "liberty" and "freedom" words so as not to sound "preachy." Above all, when "stability" doesn't cut it, the words to use are "peace" and "both sides."

Richard Boucher is a State Department professional having been in the foreign service for twenty-eight years, including posts as the U.S. ambassador to Cyprus and U.S. consul general in Hong Kong at the time of handover. He has been a spokesman for five secretaries of state of both political parties. He is a good man and one of great experience. Fortunately for his career and unfortunately for his public candor, his experience had to include schooling in the language of ambiguity. On March 8, 2005, when it was well-known that the Anti-Secession Bill of the People's Republic of China was going to be approved in six days, members of the press asked him about the pending PRC legislation that would call for potential "non-peaceful means" to be used against Taiwan by the PRC:

QUESTION: Can we move to China?
MR. BOUCHER: *Yes.*
QUESTION: Okay. Regarding the China Anti-Secession Law we saw, there is a draft and some explanation about the possible content of the law. I wonder, do you have any comment about the possible non-peaceful means to resolve Taiwan issues announced by Beijing? And especially there seems to draw a red line.
MR. BOUCHER: *Well, let me talk about a couple of things regarding this law. The full—the first is to say I don't think the full text is actually out. There has been a description of it, though, given in public and we've looked at that and we've studied that as best we can. The description given by National People's Congress Standing Committee deputy chairman Wang Zhaoguo on March 8, we think runs counter to recent trends towards a warming in cross-straits relations and we would consider passage of this law unhelpful.*

The law, as you noted, calls for non-peaceful means possibly to be directed at Taiwan. We have always opposed any attempt to determine the future of Taiwan by other than peaceful means. Our policy, I think, is well-known, but let me say again we're committed to a "one China" policy; we uphold the three communiqués; we do not support Taiwan independence.

Moreover, we oppose any attempts to unilaterally alter the status quo by either side.

We will continue to talk to both sides about these developments. We'll continue to urge both sides to avoid steps that raise tension, that risk beginning a cycle of reaction and counter-reaction, which could make dialogue more difficult.

QUESTION: A follow-up?

MR. BOUCHER: *Yes.*

QUESTION: Wang Zhaoguo seems to indicate that China could attack Taiwan if a major incident happened. You know, a change in this status quo move to Taiwan independence. Will U.S. worry that this is too ambiguous and give China, you know, a leverage of interpretation of what the status—

MR. BOUCHER: *I'm not going to try to interpret a Chinese law that we haven't seen that hasn't been passed, but certainly the kind of description of this law that we've seen, as I said, we consider unhelpful.*

We have made clear to both sides they don't—they shouldn't be taking steps right now or any time to try to unilaterally alter the situation, and that remains our position.

Yes?

QUESTION: Can you elaborate on that? You said that it was unhelpful. You then went directly into the reference to the non-peaceful means being directed at Taiwan. And now you've given a second reason, which is that you seem to suggest that the law, insofar as you understand it, would appear to be a step in the direction of resolving this unilaterally. What is your beef with the law, the non-peaceful or that you think it's a unilateral effort, or both?

MR. BOUCHER: *Both.*

QUESTION: Anything else on—

MR. BOUCHER: *No, I'll stop at that for the moment.*

QUESTION: Richard, you can't run away from the fact that the gist was—

QUESTION: A follow-up?

MR. BOUCHER: *Wait, we're—you're still on this, right?*

QUESTION: Yeah.

MR. BOUCHER: *Let him ask the question.*

QUESTION: Plus, you still can't run away from the fact that the gist of the legislation is that China would invade Taiwan if it makes any move to secede from whatever, so how would this really give any implication to the U.S. security assurances to Taiwan?

MR. BOUCHER: *We have always said that any attempt by a party to resolve this by other than peaceful means could be a threat to peace and security in the region. That's a position we've always taken and that still applies. I think the point to be made about the law—I know it's been described in various ways. The Chinese have described it as an effort for peaceful means to be used and emphasized how much it talks about peaceful attempts to reach dialogue, but they've also noted that this possibility of using non-peaceful means is in the law as well.*

I think our view would be, simply put, the two sides in different places passing laws or trying to define things is not the way this is going to be solved. This is going to be solved by the two sides getting together and talking to each other through dialogue. And passage of legislation is not going to help solve the problem. It's the peaceful dialogue that we've always supported that we think could be used to solve the problem and that's where we'd like to see the parties expending their effort.

QUESTION: What is the problem?

QUESTION: Just one quick one?

QUESTION: I mean, you say there's only one China—

MR. BOUCHER: *Yes.*

QUESTION: So the fact that the democratic island would like to wriggle—maybe wiggle free from an authoritarian government doesn't have U.S. support? What is to resolve except the absorption of Taiwan back by the mainland? Is that right?

MR. BOUCHER: *The problem is the strained relationships, the tension, the danger that exists between the people in the mainland and the people on Taiwan.*

QUESTION: The people? Well, their representatives too, no?

MR. BOUCHER: *And given the political conditions, yes.*

QUESTION: Has the U.S. expressed its concerns about the legislation directly to Chinese officials?

MR. BOUCHER: *We have. Ever since the law was being discussed, we've talked about this with people in China in the PRC as well as people on Taiwan.* [Note the use of the words "in" and "on" addressing the PRC as a nation while making Taiwan only a geographical entity.] *We've had continuing discussions with both sides and we expect that dialogue will—that discussion will continue.*

QUESTION: Has Secretary Rice talked to her counterpart about it?

MR. BOUCHER: *I'd have to check. I don't think so. I don't think this particular topic has come up, but I'd have to double-check.*

Ma'am?

QUESTION: When Secretary Rice is going to visit Beijing next week, will she raise this issue during the meeting with the Chinese leader?

MR. BOUCHER: *Well, if eventually I confirm that she's going to make a trip and that China might be part of that trip, then I would expect her to discuss Taiwan questions in Beijing if she were to go there, yes.*

QUESTION: Can I ask you about the—if you covered it, forgive me and we'll drop it. But the meeting with—

QUESTION: Richard, to come back to the Anti-Secession Law, during the discussions between the United States and China, has the United States ever raised objection to the law? And in your conversation with Taiwanese authorities, what are you telling them or urging them to do or not to do?

MR. BOUCHER: *In our contacts with both sides, we've made clear that we think that this kind of legislation is unhelpful. We've also encouraged both sides to pursue a peaceful dialogue. That's been a very consistent position of the United States.*

QUESTION: Did—sorry—quick follow-up?

MR. BOUCHER: *Yes.*

QUESTION: When Secretary Rice spoke to the Chinese foreign minister yesterday, did she raise objection to this?

MR. BOUCHER: *She talked to the Chinese foreign minister on Monday, which, in fact, was yesterday, and this subject didn't come up yesterday. I was asked if she ever raised it, and I said I'd have to check.*

Elise?

QUESTION: New topic?

MR. BOUCHER: *Nicholas?*

QUESTION: Just one quick—one thing. The ultimate goal that Beijing seeks is the peaceful unification. Is that something that you support, the unification of Taiwan with the mainland?

MR. BOUCHER: *We support peaceful dialogue to resolve the differences between Taiwan and the mainland. Where they get to in that dialogue, how they resolve those differences, will be a matter left to them.*

QUESTION: But there is only one China and Taiwan's part of it, so why wouldn't it be wrong in his assumption that you support the reunification of Taiwan with the mainland?

MR. BOUCHER: *I think he's over-interpreting or you're over-interpreting.*

I'm not sure which.

On March 24, 2005, ten days after the passage of China's Anti-Secession Law and two days before the scheduled demonstration in Taiwan in opposition to the Anti-Secession Law, the following took place at the State Department. It was a news conference with the deputy spokesman of the State Department, Adam Ereli, a foreign service officer of sixteen years who served mainly in Middle East countries and posts in D.C. He is highly regarded and received a Meritorious Honor Award and three Superior Honor Awards at the State Department:

QUESTION: Taiwan's President Chen announced that he would join the rally to protest against China's Anti-Secession Law and all his cabinet members, including the premier, as well as all their families are encouraged to join them. What do you think?

MR. ERELI: *I don't have any comment on the rally or the participants in the rally. What I would tell you is that our position is to encourage both sides to look for opportunities for dialogue and we continue to encourage both sides to avoid steps that can be seen as being unilateral or trying to resolve their differences in any way other than through dialogue.*

QUESTION: President Chen had planned to give a speech during the rally. However, he changed his mind after his meeting with a U.S. representative in Taipei. Some (inaudible) he made such a concession under U.S.—

MR. ERELI: *I wouldn't necessarily read it cause and effect to those two separate events.*

QUESTION: According to Taiwan's government official, the U.S. government will be informed as soon as President Chen's made up his mind. My question is—

MR. ERELI: *About what? About his speech?*

QUESTION: About—yeah—about he will join the rally but he will not give a speech.

MR. ERELI: *Yes.*

QUESTION: My question is, has the U.S. been informed?

MR. ERELI: *Don't know.*

That should clear things up.

CHAPTER SIXTEEN

POLITICS, POWER, PROFIT, AND LEAST OF ALL, PRINCIPLE

TAIWAN'S PRESIDENT CHEN didn't want it to happen and he made angry public statements against it, but after the trip to Beijing of Chiang Pin-kung who was the vice chairman of the Kuomintang Party, the rank of a visitor to Beijing was to go one step higher. Lien Chan, the chairman of the Kuomintang Party who was twice defeated for the presidency, accepted Beijing's invitation to visit the People's Republic of China. Chairman Lien Chan announced that he would head across the Taiwan Strait with a sixty-member delegation for an eight-day, four-city trip in China. The highlight of his itinerary would be a meeting with President Hu Jintao of the People's Republic of China.

Taiwan's President Chen was livid, as were his supporters.

The People's Republic of China had a problem, too. How could their president meet with the highest Kuomintang official coming from the "renegade province" of Taiwan and treat him as a welcome official guest? They arrived at a solution: President Hu Jintao and Lien Chan would meet as leaders of their own respective political parties, the Kuomintang and the Chinese Communist Party. That made it possible to interpret the meeting as being a visit between the heads of two political parties of "one China" or whatever people around the world wanted to think it was, as long as they didn't tell anyone.

To the total surprise of Taiwan's President Chen's supporters, President Chen suddenly made an unexpected reversal of his position of anger and made a statement of blessing Lien's forthcoming trip, exchanging a phone conversation with Lien.

President Chen's political party, the Democratic Progressive Party (DPP), was in disarray. If they supported Chen, they supported Lien's trip. If they opposed Chen, they opposed their president and the leader of their political party.

It is not uncommon in political life; some support a man over a principle and some support a principle over a man. In this case there was the accusation that President Chen bent to the pressure of the U.S. State Department.

The solved dilemma of diplomatic protocol in China and the increasing discord in Taiwan was matched by the predictable division in the government of the United States.

In defense of Lien Chan's trip to China, State Department deputy spokesman Adam Ereli said, "We believe that steps that increase dialogue, support dialogue, support a peaceful resolution of cross-strait tension are to be supported, are to be welcomed, and that's the case with this latest visit and it's, you know, we support the expansion of those kind of contacts." When asked if the steps the opposition party may take could undermine U.S. policies or change the status quo, Adam Ereli responded, "No, I don't have any comment to share with you on those discussions."

The White House spokesman, Scott McClellan, seemed to support at least part of the first sentence of the State Department statement by saying, "We welcome dialogue between Beijing and major figures in Taiwan because we believe diplomacy is the only way to resolve the cross-strait issue," then he added, "but we hope that this is the start of Beijing finding new ways to reach out to President Chen Shui-bian and his cabinet because any long-term solution can only be found if Beijing negotiates with the duly elected leadership in Taiwan." The State Department was not the author of that added statement.

By Friday, April 29, the White House, the State Department, as well as supporters and critics of Taiwan's President Chen were put into the background. It was all in the hands of chairman of the Kuomintang Party, Lien Chan, and the president of the People's Republic of China, Hu Jintao.

Amidst wine glasses, flash bulbs on digital cameras, open-mouthed smiles, and gripping handshakes, Lien Chan and Hu Jintao appeared to be in love. Even if they weren't, Lien Chan had a better reception in Beijing on this late April day than he had received in Taipei for years. And for good reason.

After a private meeting of the two, they issued a Joint Press Communiqué titled "Common Aspirations for Peaceful Cross-strait Development." (Diplomacy demands that the most interesting subjects be given the most boring names.) They agreed on "Five Tasks." (Everyone assumed they would come out with something that was numbered.) The tasks were to uphold the "Consensus of 1992," which was an unsigned and likely unwritten "consensus" defining Taiwan as part of China while each side could orally and individually define what that means through its own interpretations. In addition to upholding the Consensus of 1992 and opposing Taiwan's independence, it was stated that the "consensus" added that both sides would be seeking peace and stability across the Taiwan Strait (that's nice); promoting interchanges between both sides of the Taiwan Strait; and safeguarding the interests of the people on both sides of the Taiwan Strait. (That tear-jerking, handkerchief-wiping line adds a "How could anyone oppose this?" statement to the main item of opposing Taiwan's independence.)

One slight problem in upholding the Consensus of 1992 was that former president Lee Teng-hui said, "I was president then and there was no consensus of 1992."

Beyond the "Five Tasks," they announced that they discussed removing import duties on Taiwan's exports, liberalizing air links and shipping lanes between the two sides of the Strait, strengthening Taiwan's exports of agricultural produce to China, and establishing a common market. Then came President Hu Jintao's offer of a gift of two pandas for the Taipei zoo (to be named, by China, as Tuantuan and Yuanyuan, with even their names having a political implication, serving as a play on the Chinese word *tuanyuan,* meaning "reunion").

Lien Chan said he would urge Taiwan's president Chen and his DPP Political Party to accept the communiqué.

Lien Chan reportedly told President Hu Jintao that he would like to have an interim agreement that would last for somewhere between thirty and fifty years, mandating that during that period of time Taiwan would not declare independence while China would agree not to attack Taiwan.

It appeared to be a new version of "one country, two systems" for fifty years with Hong Kong, mixed with the "land for peace" agreement between Yasser Arafat and Israel that resulted in Israel giving up land and receiving *intifadas* (violent uprisings and terrorism) in return.

One of the highlights of Lien Chan's visit to China was his speech at Beijing University when he called both the National Taiwan University and Beijing University "fortresses and front guards of liberalism." (Some of Beijing University's students were massacred and some of the alumni were still in prison for participating in the 1989 demonstration in Tiananmen Square, asking for dialogue and democracy.)

Something unexpected happened when Lien went to Nanjing. Among the crowd greeting him was one brave man who held up a banner that read, "Restore the Republic of China! Marxism is the greatest evil in the world!" Police quickly took him away and what happened to him is, at this writing, unknown.

After eight days Lien Chan came back home to Taipei to an anti-Lien Chan demonstration of thousands in what was called a "Night to Oppose War and Protect Taiwan" critical of Lien for "denigrating Taiwan and currying favor with China."

Taiwan's president Chen Shui-bian invited China's president Hu Jintao to Taiwan to experience democracy and freedom and to see for himself "if Taiwan is a country with independent sovereignty." As with past invitations for presidents of China to visit Taiwan, President Hu Jintao refused and would only visit Taiwan if President Chen first "recognized Chinese sovereignty over Taiwan," with "reunification under the 'one China' policy."

Within days, James Soong of Taiwan's minority People First Party, which was part of the Pan-Blue coalition with the Kuomintang, emphasized his opposition to Taiwan independence and that he, like Lien Chan, would now accept the invitation of China to visit with its leaders.

He made the trip and said in Shanghai, "The People First Party is firmly against Taiwan's independence. Taiwan independence has never been our option. That will only bring wars and unnecessary disasters. We hope both sides can build markets and factories, and not become a battleground."

More important than Taiwan's Lien Chan and James Soong, who were not in office, was the leader of Taiwan, President Chen Shui-bian, who back at home was continuing to give conflicting signals of vacillation from his earlier statements when he had opposed unofficial visits by representatives of political parties that had lost at the ballot box. He now said, "In striving to develop Taiwan's external relations, we cannot rely on just the Democratic Progressive Party. The role of the opposition parties is equally important." He added that as long as the opposition leaders did not violate the law, he preferred to view the visits to China from a "more lenient perspective" rather than a partisan view:

"The door for dialogue and negotiation is still open between the two sides [Taiwan and China]. Under the principles of democracy, peace, and parity, the two sides can at any time begin to have contact, dialogue, and negotiation…[Lien Chan] kept his promise not to sign any pact there…I have given James Soong a message to carry to President Hu Jintao…"

Legislators from the president's party, the Democratic Progressive Party, responded one after the other to the wavering comments of President Chen:

Legislator Kuo Cheng-liang said, "As a president it is not the way to do things."

Legislator Jao Yung-ching said, "We realize that the president's recent remarks have indeed created some trouble for the party…"

Legislator Lee Wen-chung said, "I personally think that the president is not acting like a president and the government is not acting like a government."

Legilator Wang Sing-nan said:"I have received so many telephone calls from my voters, cursing at us, the party, and President Chen. The president must respond to those complaints. If he finds turning the country into a normal and independent sovereign state a burden, he might want to consider withdrawing from the party."

"My views on Taiwan's sovereignty and future haven't changed," President Chen answered back. He said that opposition party leaders like Lien Chan and James Soong "can shake hands with the Chinese leader, but I can't because we can't give up our insistence on Taiwan sovereignty, equality, and dignity."

It sounded principled if his remarks of only days earlier were disregarded. But they were difficult to disregard.

A *Taipei Times* editorial wrote in part:

> Amid the recent wave of China fever, Chen put his foot down by threatening to harshly deal with anyone who violated the law. But days later he is full of "blessing, support, and recognition" for the opposition leaders. He even gave the impression that a Chen-Hu meeting could be held as soon as Hu snaps his fingers...All of this indicates that if Chen betrays the people of Taiwan by walking down a red carpet rolled out by China, the curtain will go down on his political career.

On the other side of Taiwan's political spectrum there was no gratitude for President Chen's extended hand. It soon became known that what was said during discussions that were held in Beijing between opposition leaders and officials of the People's Republic of China was to be kept secret by the Taiwan opposition parties. Joseph Wu, the head of Taiwan's Mainland Affairs Council, said, "We asked for the official transcripts of the meetings, but we received no reply. We debated whether our laws on treason apply in this case. But we decided charges would bring harm and greater chaos. We are a democracy and so it is best that we act like one."

It was widely reported that a senior People First Party legislator, Nelson Ku, who went to Beijing with James Soong, responded to a request for transcripts by answering, "I'm sorry, we can't share this with [the president of Taiwan] Chen Shui-bian. We don't trust him."

To other countries of the world, as well as to his own people, it was difficult to know the beliefs of President Chen, and what President Chen would advocate next. In contrast, his two-term vice president, Annette Hsiu-lien Lu, retained convictions that did not waver even while inconsistency was becoming the legacy of President Chen. At the same time, opposition parties and their unelected politicians were engaged in such extreme national disunity that Taiwan's democracy could be the loser, with the "renegade province" in time becoming a captured province of the People's Republic of China. Such disunity could bring such capture about without the launch of one missile from across the Taiwan Strait or the use of a blockade or an invasion.

Decades back, similar disunity in the United States brought about the defeat of South Vietnam, Cambodia, and Laos. In the current decade the United States is suffering from political domestic disunity in fighting the war against Islamist terrorism.

There are, of course, in every country, the disunited who will accept peace at any price. Those are the ones who do not know that liberty without peace still has hope, while peace without liberty is surrender. Always.

In the conflict between the People's Republic of China and Taiwan, disunity is running rampant: President Chen Shui-bian craves approval from everyone; Taiwan's major out-of-power politicians crave power; profiteers throughout the world crave business in China; and the United States craves a policy of ambiguity. All of that provides a mix with conflicting objectives, while the People's Republic of China has one clear goal—it wants Taiwan.

CHAPTER SEVENTEEN

A SHORT TRIP

IT WAS SCHEDULED to be one of those tedious meetings that particular world leaders feel they have to attend every year. No one looks forward to these things except some of the staff people of those world leaders who can see places they haven't seen before and make up stories about the great things that were accomplished at the meeting. This one was the Asian Pacific Economic Conference (APEC) taking place in Busan [Pusan], South Korea, in November 2005.

President George W. Bush was one of the "Do I have to?" world leaders who were on their way to the dreary routine. In a wise bit of scheduling, President Bush would stop off at Kyoto in Japan before getting to the hard-to-endure meeting, and then after the meeting there was an unwise bit of scheduling for the president to go to Beijing for a time of tenseness and diplomatic juggling. And finally there would be the destination of Ulan Bator in Mongolia, like dessert after the main dish was done.

In Kyoto he was praising economic freedom, which was appropriate since he was en route to an economic conference, but then he added something that was surprising: he gave Taiwan as an example of economic liberalization and didn't stop there. He added:

> Modern Taiwan is free and democratic and prosperous. By embracing freedom at all levels, Taiwan has delivered prosperity to its people and created a free and democratic Chinese society. Our 'one China' policy remains unchanged. It is based on the three communiqués, the Taiwan Relations Act, and our belief that there should be no unilateral attempts to change the status quo by either side. The United States will continue to stress the need for dialogue between China and Taiwan that leads to a peaceful resolution of their differences.

Much of his statement was worthy of applause, but it had to have been written by a committee, as it allowed any foreign power or any one anywhere to pick the words needed to prove that the president feels the same as the person who is trying to prove a point.

The Taiwan advocate could quote, "Modern Taiwan is free and democratic and prosperous. By embracing freedom at all levels, Taiwan has delivered prosperity to its people and created a free and democratic...society." [Actually he said "a free and democratic *Chinese* society" but it isn't a Chinese society; it's a Taiwanese society.] "Our...policy is based on...the Taiwan Relations Act...The United States will continue to stress the need for dialogue between China and Taiwan that leads to a peaceful resolution of their differences."

The People's Republic of China advocate could say President Bush said that Taiwan is a "Chinese society...Our 'one China' policy remains unchanged. It is based on the three communiqués...and our belief that there should be no unilateral attempts to change the status quo...The United States will continue to stress the need for dialogue between China and Taiwan that leads to a...resolution."

Such excerpts by either advocate would be unfair, but they could be used, and within days they had been used.

After the APEC meeting was done in Busan, South Korea, the president went on to Beijing. His most recent meeting with the People's Republic of China's president Hu Jintao had been brief, just two months earlier in New York at the Waldorf Astoria when both presidents were in New York for the sixtieth anniversary of the U.N. In that meeting, both presidents had appeared at what was meant to be a photo opportunity and a welcome to the United States by President Bush and a gracious thank-you by President Hu. It did work out that way, except that President Hu went on to make a speech that included: "The proper handling of the Taiwan question holds the key to sound and steady growth of the China-U.S. relationship. President Bush has, on various occasions, stated his commitment to the 'one China' policy, the three Sino-U.S. joint communiqués, and opposition to so-called Taiwan independence, which I highly appreciate. I hope that the United States will join the

Chinese side in safeguarding peace and stability across the Taiwan Straits, and opposing so-called Taiwan independence."

Once in Beijing, President Bush met with President Hu Jintao at the Great Hall of the People on the edge of Tiananmen Square, just as President Clinton had met with President Jiang Zemin in 1998. The only difference was that President Hu Jintao did not allow a joint news conference with the U.S. president and the international press. Instead, prepared comments were given with President Hu saying, "We will by no means tolerate Taiwan independence."

President Bush did not respond to that but instead thanked President Hu for "taking the lead" in the Six-Power (United States, Japan, Russia, South Korea, North Korea, and China) Nuclear Disarmament Talks regarding North Korea. It was a deft and revealing transition of dialogue that might have indicated something beyond a quick change of subject.

The following is only speculative: President Bush is more than aware that President Hu cannot be counted on to conclude a successful resolution of North Korea's nuclear ambitions. President Bush is not naïve, nor unaware of North Korea's history under Kim Jong Il or under Kim Jong Il's father, Kim Il Sung. Through the entire history of the People's Republic of China and the Democratic People's Republic of Korea (North Korea), the two governments have been close allies in both wars and peace. (And, not so incidentally, the killing of U.S. armed forces.)

Having a successful resolution coming from the Six-Power Talks is, most likely, not why the United States wants China involved in the Six-Party Talks. Instead, there is the hope that China's involvement in the talks can act as a delaying tactic that is believed to be preferable to any immediate crises while our plate is full.

An agreement made with North Korea might well be more harmful to the United States than not having any agreement at all, since the North Korean government has no hesitancy to sign an international agreement with every intention of violating its own signature. Its history of agreements is filled with deception as recently as those accords signed during the Clinton administration. Prime among them was the 1994 Advanced Framework Agreement that called for North Korea to freeze its nuclear weapons program and allow the International Atomic Energy Agency [IAEA] safeguards if the United

States, Japan, and South Korea would provide two light-water nuclear plants that were "proliferation-resistant" to replace its graphite-moderated nuclear plants. (It had been initiated months earlier by former president Jimmy Carter who went to Pyongyang, North Korea, and had two days of discussions with President Kim Il Sung.)

Back then, all sides agreed that the United States would provide fuel oil pending the construction of the reactors (as well as other aid to North Korea). Eight years later, in 2002, North Korean officials admitted that during those eight years they had been engaged in a clandestine program of uranium enrichment that could be used to build nuclear weapons, and in 2003 North Korea expelled the IAEA inspectors. In a 2003 discussion, this one with the United States and China in Beijing, North Korean officials said they possessed nuclear weapons.

After such a history, any further agreement with the North Korean government would be totally devoid of credibility.

But it is believed to be tremendously useful to have China "take the lead" in the Six-Power Talks, with China's Hu Jintao knowing exactly why we are doing what we are doing. It makes no difference that the North Koreans cancel the talks, then re-enter them, cancel them again, then re-enter them again. The longer diplomacy goes on, it is thought to be better than what might be the immediate alternative. But it leaves Kim Jong Il the master of his schedule.

The time delay may be wise, but attempted delaying tactics and time consumption with tyrannies generally appear to be helpful in the short term but not in the reality of the long term. President Johnson's thirteen bombing pauses of North Vietnam consumed time and gave relief to much of the public, but gave the North Vietnamese thirteen occasions to build up its forces along the Ho Chi Minh Trail. Our time consumption in going through the U.N. for seventeen resolutions against Saddam Hussein's Iraq was positive in terms of temporary public perceptions, but gave Saddam Hussein a decade of opportunities to prepare for what was inevitable by the U.S. and not the U.N.

China's reward for its role in the Six-Power Talks is the hope of ultimately intoxicating President Bush into feeling obligated to give in to a policy of reciprocity regarding the PRC's obsession of conquering Taiwan.

And so we have Presidents Bush and Hu together with President Hu saying, "We will by no means tolerate Taiwan independence," and President Bush ignoring the comment, not intoxicated into a policy of reciprocity, but giving instead appreciation for President Hu "taking the lead" in the Six-Power Nuclear Disarmament Talks with North Korea.

Rather unexpectedly President Bush also said, "We encourage the Chinese to continue to make an historic transition to greater freedom."

President Bush had with him a list of names of political prisoners President Bush wanted released by President Hu, the names having first been given to President Hu by President Bush two months earlier when they met in New York. The prisoners were still not released.

It was Sunday and President Bush went to the Gangwashi Church, one of the few state-approved and monitored Protestant churches, its congregation required to register with the government as part of its "Three Self Patriotic Movement."

President Bush signed the guest book with the inscription, "May God Bless the Christians of China."

CHAPTER EIGHTEEN

CHAIRMAN MA
SMILES A LOT

MORE BAD LUCK for Taiwan's President Chen: the 2005 elections in Taiwan were scheduled for December 3 at a time when polls indicated that President Chen's popularity had moved even lower than before, floating around 25 percent. Fortunately for President Chen, the December 3 elections were only local, and would not include the election of a president (scheduled for 2008) or even an election of Taiwan's legislators, but it came at a time when many elements were moving against his Democratic Progressive Party, including disapproval from his own base of independence-supporters for his inconsistencies on cross-strait issues.

The elections were called "Three in One," which were to be elections of township executives, city and county executives, and municipal councils. Their importance, however, was magnified because this was an internationally watched opportunity for most of the country to go to the polls and indicate their approval or disapproval of the Democratic Progressive Party. (The cities of Taipei and Kaohsiung were excluded from the December 3 elections since their mayors and city council members were scheduled for election the following year, 2006.) It seemed as though things couldn't get better for the Kuomintang Party until things *did* get better for the Kuomintang.

Something happened that often happens in democracies before elections: the major opposition party gets hold of a scandal in the other major party and runs with it—and in this case there was a scandal with which to run. The unraveling of the scandal started in August. First, it was about Thai workers in Taiwan who rioted against what they said were inhumane working conditions on the mass rapid-transit system they were constructing in Kaohsiung,

Taiwan. It got worse. Allegedly, photographs were revealed show-ing Chen Che-nan, the deputy secretary general of the President's Office, on a gambling trip to South Korea, with the accusation that the trip was financed by either representatives or friends of that mass rapid-transit firm that was constructing the transit system in Kaohsiung. The allegations were made that Chen Che-nan was re-sponsible for the miserable conditions, bending the rules for the transit system in return for gifts given him, including the gambling trip. He denied the accusations.

All the accusations resulted in twenty-one people being in-dicted, including Chen Che-nan, who was expelled from his posi-tion of deputy secretary general of the President's Office. This laby-rinthine story of corruption could, of course, further damage Presi-dent Chen Shui-bian's Democratic Progressive Party candidates in the coming local elections.

It was a terrible defeat for the Democratic Progressive Party. All in all, the Kuomintang took 51 percent of the vote and the Democratic Progressive Party took 42 percent. The Kuomintang won fourteen offices, up from eight, while its Pan-Blue allies won three more. The Democratic Progressive Party won only six offices, down from nine.

President Chen wrote in his electronic newsletter, "It feels terri-ble to face a lost election. But this is the decision of the people."

The Kuomintang enhanced its December 3 election victories by claiming a hero: the man who had taken over the chairmanship of the Kuomintang Party just three months earlier; Ma Ying-jeou.

In that one day, Chairman Ma was raised to the stature of the Kuomintang's almost-certain candidate for the presidency in 2008. (The nominee of the Democratic Progressive Party in the 2008 presi-dential election was unknown and unpredicted to follow President Chen Shui-bian who, by law, was prohibited from seeking a third term.) Chairman Ma was the fifty-five-year-old mayor of Taipei who was elected to that office in 1998 and reelected in 2002. There was wide agreement that he was charismatic and politically adept.

He had all the qualifications for the Kuomintang. He was one year old when his family brought him from Hong Kong to Taiwan. His family was strongly Kuomintang. His educational background included Harvard University. Later he entered the political life of Taiwan as an ardent Kuomintang advocate.

President Lee Teng-hui (who at that time was also Kuomintang) appointed him justice minister in 1993. He was told to leave his post in 1996. In 1998 he ran for mayor of Taipei against the incumbent mayor, Chen Shui-bian (the future president), who was running for reelection as mayor. Ma won 51 percent of the votes and four years later ran for reelection himself, this time winning the mayor's race by a landslide 64 percent.

Now there was the landslide of his party in local elections of December of 2006, and he was in the ideal spot as the new chairman of the Kuomintang. When he took over the party he praised his predecessor, Lien Chan, for his travel to Beijing and said, "I will do my best to carry on and push for Lien Chan's policies."

Eleven days after the Kuomintang's victory in the December 3 elections, a meeting with an American was held with Chairman Ma in his mayor's office. Since the meeting was not audiotaped, the dialogue that follows is not written with word-by-word precision, but it is as close as possible.

The guest from the United States told Chairman Ma that many of the most ardent long-time supporters of Taiwan in Washington, D.C., were becoming less supportive because of the actions of his Kuomintang political party.

The guest asked Chairman Ma if he would explain a number of Kuomintang actions:

1. After the Anti-Secession law was passed in Beijing and a demonstration against that law was held in Taipei with some one million people participating, there were no leaders of the Kuomintang (KMT) taking part in that demonstration.

2. Very quickly after the passage of the Anti-Secession Bill there were travels of Kuomintang (KMT) leaders to Beijing.

3. There were 41 rejections of the Defense Procurement Bill, the rejections led by the KMT, although the KMT had been supportive of those U.S. defenses for Taiwan while the KMT held the presidency.

4. His KMT political party didn't want a name change of the nation or even a name change of public enterprises to the name of Taiwan.

5. His party was opposed to independence, and made that clear in Beijing.

6. His party wanted a "reunification" with China.

In short, his party was advocating policies of the PRC. It was asked, why embrace the one and only power that has massed arms against the people of Taiwan, and warns they could be used?

Chairman Ma answered that although the KMT didn't participate in the demonstration, city mayors (himself included) and county magistrates issued an open letter of protest against the Anti-Secession Law. He asked his secretary to bring in a copy of the letter. While she was getting it, he answered some of the other points including the one on defense, saying there was a referendum on the issue that the people of Taiwan rejected.

"They did?"

"Ah, you didn't know that?"

"No, I didn't."

"It lost."

"Wait...wait a minute. Are you talking about the referendum in 2004?"

"That's right."

"Mayor Ma, it was approved by over 80 percent of the voters—but because of the rule that made it necessary for more than 50 percent of the registered voters having to cast ballots, it didn't pass."

"They didn't participate because we [the KMT] boycotted it. We were opposed to the referendum."

Chairman Ma exposed what he had not planned on volunteering but he knew to be true; that those who voted were overwhelming in their support of the questions asked in the referendum. (The two questions asked of the voters in that referendum were as written in Chapter Eight.) Eighty-seven percent of the voters voted yes on both questions, including the question on defense. Chairman Ma's answer regarding the boycott of the KMT was not convincing. Boycotts of elections and boycotts of plebiscites are commonly used by those who feel their side will be rejected by the voters, so as to be able to say the boycott was the reason for the election results. The Marxist guerrillas boycotted elections in El Salvador in 1982 and the Sunnis boycotted elections in Iraq in January 2005. In both cases, they could then claim their side would have won had they participated. In future elections when they did participate, they lost.

Later in the meeting Chairman Ma spoke about the Kuomintang Party's problem in voting for the Defense Procurement Bill since his party believed that money should not come from a new procurement bill but from the appropriations already in the annual defense budget. When he was reminded that those processes can be changed and that it is just a procedural matter that has nothing to do with what's needed, he answered that the defense items that are called for in the bill are out of date with what is needed. But there was no Kuomintang bill for what they believed to be "in-date." The Defense Procurement Bill (already rejected forty-one times and rejected fifteen more times by the end of June 2006) was to accept the United States' offer of six Patriot PAC-3 Missile Defense System batteries, eight diesel-powered submarines, and twelve P-3C Orion anti-submarine aircraft. (The People's Republic of China has approximately a hundred submarines. Taiwan has four submarines, two of them from the era of World War II.)

The Kuomintang would not allow the Defense Procurement Bill to be taken up or discussed in committee. To make it more acceptable to the Kuomintang, the package was continually lowered in terms of size and price from $18 billion to $15 billion to $11 billion, and still it was rejected by the narrow majority of Pan-Blue parties led by the Kuomintang, claiming the package was too expensive, unnecessary, and against the wishes of the people. President Chen offered to meet Ma Ying-jeou to discuss what he *would* approve, and Ma Ying-jeou would not schedule such a meeting.

The conversation then shifted to Chairman Ma's major issue—his belief in economic advantages for Taiwan in doing business with China; increasing trade and investment across the Taiwan Strait. As is so frequently true, representatives defending the KMT turn to economics rather than the subject of sustaining liberty and democracy. It was brought to his attention that many Taiwanese businesspeople and their lust for increased profits are threatening Taiwan's existence by becoming dependent on China, and the American remarked that China is obsessed with taking over Taiwan.

He shook his head, saying that "no longer is the PRC focusing on or pushing for Taiwan's unification with the mainland." His statement was surprising to hear since just nine months earlier Beijing had passed the Anti-Secession Law with its warning of employing "non-peaceful means" should Taiwan reject "peaceful reunification." (Eight months after this meeting, China's ambassador to the U.N., Sha Kukang, told the BBC that if Taiwan should declare independence, "It is not a question of how big Taiwan is. For China, one inch of territory is more valuable than the life of our people.")

By this time of the meeting with Mayor Ma, his secretary arrived with the letter that city mayors, including Mayor Ma, and county magistrates of the ROC issued. The letter, issued in response to the Anti-Secession Law, was titled, "Taiwan Believes in Peace and Dialogue. An Open Letter to the International Community to Protest Mainland China's Anti-Secession Law." Indeed, it protested the law and protested it strongly. There were, however, lines in the letter (those lines printed here in italics) that were questionable at best. The entire letter follows:

> Today, the National People's Congress of the People's Republic of China (PRC) passed the Anti-Secession Law targeting Taiwan. This move has provoked strong reaction from Taiwanese people, caused concern in the international community, and cast a new variable into an already delicate cross-strait relationship.
>
> As city mayors and county magistrates of the Republic of China (ROC) we have gathered here to make a clear statement to the world and to register our discontent and protest on behalf of the grassroots citizens of Taiwan.
>
> We maintain that *Mainland* China should clearly understand that the Republic of China has been a sovereign state since 1912, and that status remains unchanged. The majority of Taiwan's citizens support maintaining the status quo. *True, a minority of people in Taiwan advocate independence and wish to adopt a constitution and change the country's name. But they are not the voice of the majority in Taiwan.* ROC President Chen Shui-bian has declared publicly that changing the country's

name by adopting a new constitution is not possible, and Premier Frank Hsieh has pointed out that the government must abide by the "One China Constitution." *Taiwan, itself, has laws that prohibit the secession of national territory.*

Mainland China's enacting of the Anti-Secession Law in response to a minority view in Taiwan clearly ignores Taiwan's mainstream opinion. The move is neither necessary nor wise; it has provoked strong objection from the Taiwanese people, and it clouds the future development of cross-strait relations. *Taiwan must maintain its status as the Republic of China* — this is the common ground between the opposition and ruling parties, and the key to lowering cross-strait tension.

Mainland China and Taiwan have been separated and under separate rule since 1949. *Mainland* China has never administered Taiwan, and the Republic of China's current jurisdiction does not extend to the Chinese *mainland*. All political issues must therefore be resolved through peaceful negotiations on an equal footing. Such good faith negotiations between the two sides can only proceed while two fundamental premises are observed: *Mainland* China does not use force against Taiwan, and *Taiwan does not declare independence.*

Unfortunately, the National People's Congress has unilaterally passed the Anti-Secessionist Law. The law is a domestic one and is intended to "internalize" the cross-strait dispute, leaving open the possibility of resolving the issue by "nonpeaceful" means. This approach damages mutual trust and limits the ability of both sides to peaceably resolve political conflict. It is indeed unnecessary and unwise. We must therefore solemnly register our discontent and protest.

Stability in the Taiwan Strait is vital to the peace and security of East Asia, and depends upon the efforts of the authorities across the Taiwan Strait to jointly demonstrate, by their actions, their determination to achieve peace. The cross-strait chartered flights during Chinese New Year early this year demonstrated the successful reconciliation between the two sides. We therefore call upon the authorities of Taiwan and *Mainland* China to honor this window of opportunity, and to face and solve the problems soberly and objectively. We regret the enactment of the Anti-Secession Law, but we do not wish to see the two sides pursue a course of emotional confrontation. We therefore request the immediate resumption of dialogue to negotiate the issues on an equal footing. By

pursuing dialogue earnestly and openly, we can together ensure the welfare of the people on both sides and preserve
peace in the Taiwan Strait in conformity with the wishes of
the international community.

*We hope that the international community understands the present
situation of Taiwan's mainstream opinion and the key to solving
the cross-strait problems.*

We also hope the international community will encourage
and help the two sides to resume peaceful and equal negotiations on the basis of the status quo. This will favor the welfare of the people and the stability of the region. We call
upon the *Mainland* authorities to forswear unilaterally solving cross-strait problems by non-peaceful means. *We hope
that our central government will adopt a more practical and rational stance in order to realize peace, and to actively promote dialogue and negotiation across the Taiwan Strait.*

It should be noted that the continual use of the word *mainland*
suggests that Taiwan is indeed part of China, although many inad-
vertently use that expression from force of habit.

The most significant revelation of the meeting between Chairman Ma and the American visitor was that Chairman Ma totally
ignored the statement by the American that many of the most ardent long-time supporters of Taiwan in Washington, D.C., were
becoming less supportive because of the actions of his Kuomintang
Party. Indisputably that statement would bother any advocate of
Taiwan and it was obvious that it was true, yet he did not seem
bothered by it, nor did he address it.

Because of the actions of the Kuomintang and because of the
victory in the local elections, the entire issue of Taiwan can be put
into two questions:

1. Will the *Taiwanese* risk war with China to retain their
    democracy?

2. Will the *United States* risk war with China to retain the
    democracy of the Taiwanese?

The answer to the second question will be dependent on the answer to the first question. The Kuomintang would surely not risk war

with China to retain a democracy. Democracy is the enemy of the Kuomintang Party. Democracy expelled the Kuomintang from presidential power. The Kuomintang would not have lost presidential power if the 2000 and 2004 free elections did not take place. That must be remembered by citizens of Taiwan and the United States: the Kuomintang came to power without democracy and lost that power in the 2000 election after President Lee, the unique Kuomintang democracy-advocate who won the first direct election for the presidency did not run again. (He later quit the Kuomintang as its pro-China policies increased.) The threat democracy presented to the Kuomintang's continuing anti-democratic authoritarian power did not pass unnoticed by the Kuomintang's leaders. If they favor democracy why did they oppose and even boycott the referendum of 2004 that would express the will of the people? (As mentioned earlier, Chairman Ma proudly stated to his American visitor that the Kuomintang opposed the referendum and boycotted it.)

But in the elections of leaders, the Kuomintang knew they had to play the game if they wanted any chance of regaining power. The local elections of December 3, 2005, gave them confidence they might be able to go further and win national elections, including the presidency by 2008. They needed an electable candidate, and they needed to continue playing on the fear of war from the PRC if Taiwan should adopt policies that were disapproved by the PRC. On the economic front, they needed to convince the electorate that without trade and investment in the PRC, the income of Taiwanese citizens would suffer.

If Chairman Ma should win the presidency it would not be at all surprising that before the end of his term or terms in office, Taiwan would be scheduled to live under a "one country, two systems" structure. The reward for the Kuomintang would be the promises of power from Beijing. For those who don't believe this, look to Beijing to find out if it favors Pan-Green or Pan-Blue policies. If someone doesn't know, then that person should write a list of those policies Beijing wants the people of Taiwan to reject (such as putting to a vote whether or not to change the name from the Republic of China; changing the names of public enterprises; rewriting the constitution should the people of Taiwan vote for changes in the constitution; other referenda for the people's approval or disapproval; abolition of the National Unification [with China] Council; the purchase of defense items from the United States or elsewhere; Taiwanese appearing in demonstrations that protest Beijing's warnings of non-peaceful means to unify; or independence—or add anything else that is opposed by Beijing). Next to the list of items that the Beijing government wants the people of Taiwan to reject, write a list of those policies the Kuomintang wants the people of Taiwan to reject.

There will be an obvious similarity in the two lists. That similarity is not coincidental. The Kuomintang has taken the role of being a proxy for major policies of the People's Republic of China.

CHAPTER NINETEEN

NEW YEAR'S RESOLUTIONS

COLLEAGUES AND FELLOW CITIZENS: Good morning and a Happy New Year to all of you!" It was Taiwan's president Chen on January 1, 2006, delivering the most unexpected and the best speech of his career:

> The emergence of Taiwan consciousness and a wave of democratization have galvanized the aspiration of the Taiwan people to be masters of their own land...The world's tallest skyscraper—Taipei 101—towers majestically over its capital. Yet it is grievously saddening that circumstances forbid us from saying out loud consistently the name of our country— such is indeed a heartbreaking and humiliating predicament...

> We must say to the world, loud and clear, that the ultimate decision on Taiwan's future must—and will—be made by the 23 million people of Taiwan, by their own free will. Their freedom to choose the path they want to take cannot be denied by the unilateral adoption of a so-called Anti-Secession Law by the Chinese National People's Congress, which calls for resorting to the use of non-peaceful means; nor can our civil liberties be seized through military intimidation and belligerent rhetoric.

> At present, the Chinese People's Liberation Army (PLA) has deployed 784 ballistic missiles targeting Taiwan along the coast across the Taiwan Strait; the PRC has also vigorously reinforced its naval and air force combat readiness, coordinating its ground, information, electronics, and Special Forces, severely impacting and imposing a direct threat to peace in the Taiwan Strait...

Following China's so-called "annihilation" of the Republic of China in 1949, it has unceasingly pursued its ambition to annex Taiwan.

Recent reports on the military power of the People's Republic of China, published by the United States and Japan respectively, have made it very clear that China's military development evidently exceeds the reasonable scope of its defense needs. In the face of such imminent and obvious threat, Taiwan must not rest its fate on chance or harbor any illusions...I would like to once again, with utmost sincerity, call upon opposition leaders and party caucuses to be more rational and to reconsider allowing the arms procurement bill to be sent to the full legislature for deliberation. With regard to reducing the budget or how the special budget or annual budget may be adjusted, the executive branch will respect the opinions of the Legislative Yuan; however, there should be no more excuses to cause further delays. Citizens should also be engaged in voicing their concerns on Taiwan's national defense budget—to which the personal security of every individual is inextricably linked—so as to serve as proactive overseers by putting pressure on the executive and legislative branches to shoulder their due responsibilities to national security...

We will harness the collective wisdom and fortitude of our citizens to produce "Taiwan's New Constitution" by 2008— one that is timely, relevant, and viable...The journey may be arduous, but if we have faith, if we persist, we will find a way...

No matter how insurmountable the setbacks and challenges, we shall not despair, but hold fast and tread onward with courage. Taiwan is our homeland forever, and the hope of our future generations.

President Chen also made a point of apologizing for the scandal that had dominated Taiwan news prior to the December 3 election: "A few former members of the administration in the past have been charged with inappropriate conduct, causing disappointment to those who had high expectations of us. I take it upon myself to shoulder all the blame and to once again express my apology to all our fellow citizens."

President Chen later defined how he envisioned the process for a new constitution: a draft of a new constitution should be completed by the end of 2006, then put to a popular vote in 2007, and if the people approve the draft of the constitution, it would take effect on May 20, 2008, the day he leaves office.

In Southern Taiwan on the Lunar New Year, President Chen added a new significant statement regarding relations between Taiwan and China: "There are people urging that the National Unification Council and its guidelines be abolished. I think now is the appropriate time we must seriously consider it—take a good look at it." The National Unification Council had been established in 1990 by the Kuomintang, its guidelines established in 1991. The council was formed to establish plans for the unification of China and Taiwan.

Since the Democratic Progressive Party took the presidency in 2000 there had not been any meetings of the council. President Chen continued, "This is an extremely serious topic. As everybody knows all that's left of the council is a name. This kind of council and its representatives seek a unified China, and under the guidelines even accepts the 'one China' principle. These are all problems."

In short time, Chairman Ma responded to President Chen's remarks: "President Chen promised that he would not abolish the National Unification Council and GNU [guidelines of the council] when he became president in 2000 and when he won a second term in 2004. Chen's honesty will be further questioned and he will pay for breaking his promise."

The *China Post*, a Taiwan newspaper supportive of the Kuomintang, added: "The risk is tremendous. Should it become apparent that neither Taiwan's own opposition forces nor its U.S. defense ally could come up with effective countermeasures to contain Chen in his provocative political programs, it might eventually prompt Beijing to take action against Taiwan invoking the 2005 law that authorizes the communist People's Liberation Army to invade this island if it persistently pushes for formal independence."

(In other words, the subliminal message is clear: if Taiwan's people don't support the Kuomintang, there could be war.)

The subject quickly became an international issue with Russia's Foreign Ministry issuing a statement: "His [President Chen's] intention to liquidate the National Reunification Council and give up the program of national reunification indicates that the Taiwanese leadership is not interested in building constructive dialogue with the mainland. This may be regarded as a movement towards the independence of Taiwan. To the best of our knowledge, such steps are at variance with expectations of the majority of people in Taiwan. Not only do they fail to pursue the interests of maintaining peace and stability, but they are also fraught with serious considerations for the Asia Pacific region as a whole…[Russia firmly believes that] there is only one China in the world, and Taiwan is its inalienable part, expressly stated in the Russian-Chinese Treaty of Good Neighborliness, Friendship, and Cooperation of July 16, 2001, and in a number of Russian-Chinese documents, and is not subject to change."

Across the strait from Taiwan, China's president Hu Jintao made his own New Year's resolution. After the negative world reaction to China's Anti-Secession Law early in the preceding year, China employed a new and more sophisticated technique. Hu Jintao's New Year's resolution was the opposite of President Chen's resolution.

Whereas Taiwan's President Chen had been too gentle on China and Taiwan bore the consequences, and he was now changing to a stronger course, President Hu, who had consistently warned Taiwan to the point of threatening war, was now acting as though Taiwan had already agreed to be part of China. He had previewed his course at the end of 2005 with the offer of gifts of pandas; inviting an increase in investment for Taiwan businesspeople; loans to Taiwanese businesspeople; charter flights for Taiwanese to come to China during the Lunar New Year, which had been done annually since 2003 but now increased to thirty-six flights; additional charter flights for other major holidays; importing agricultural goods from Taiwan; willingness to establish three direct links for trade, transport, and postal services; scholarships for Taiwanese students in China; and directing the Olympic torch to go through Taiwan in the torch relay for the 2008 Beijing Olympic Games. (There was a hitch here. China intended for this to be a domestic stop of the torch while Taiwan wanted it to be an international stop.)

The U.S State Department made no New Year's resolution at all. It issued its usual statement emphasizing that the United States "does not support Taiwan's independence and opposes unilateral changes to the status quo by either Taiwan or Beijing." At the news briefing in which the statement was read, Adam Ereli, the deputy spokesman for the State Department, added in explanation, "We're issuing this in the wake of some comments by President Chen in Taiwan that we don't want to be inflammatory or send the wrong signal, so we thought it useful to reiterate U.S. policy on the subject."

A reporter asked, "What do you think of his move to abolish the unification panel that was set up?"

"Well, as I said, there were some remarks over the weekend that are just that—remarks. As far as U.S. is concerned—United States is concerned, our policy towards this issue hasn't changed. We think it's important that both sides engage in dialogue and that there be—and very importantly, I think it's—I want to underscore this—the United States opposes any unilateral change to the status quo by either side."

"On Taiwan too, the—President Chen also mentioned that he would like to promote Taiwan's participation in the United Nations, especially in the name of Taiwan. I'm just wondering, what's the U.S. stand on that issue?"

"I think if you look at the broad principles of our policy, you'll see that we don't—we oppose, as I just said, any unilateral change to the status quo, and that would govern that issue as well."

"About the United Nations participation?"

"That's a unilateral change to the status quo."

Taiwan's president Chen, in January 2006, became a president with coherent principles. But not for long. Clifford Hart of the U.S. State Department and Dennis Wilder of the National Security Council came to Taipei and met with President Chen. Soon thereafter, the State Department's Adam Ereli said that Taiwan should "publicly correct the record and unambiguously affirm it did not abolish the National Unification Council, did not change the status quo, and that the assurances remain in effect."

President Chen then disowned "abolition" by saying that the National Unification Council has "ceased to function" and its guidelines have "ceased to apply." Others in his administration explained that the word "abolition" was a fault in translation, and since the council had not met since 2000 when President Chen took office then, factually, it did cease to function and its guidelines did cease to apply, and that President Chen was merely stating facts.

That didn't make China any happier. Chinese premier Wen Jiabo called President Chen's words "extremely dangerous and deceptive. We need to stay alert to the fact they are now intensifying their secessionist activities. We are closely following developments and we are fully prepared for all the eventualities."

D.C. diplomats regarded President Chen's new "translation" from "abolition" of the National Unification Council to "ceased to function" as a victory since weeks of discussion changed the wording from what was considered to be unacceptable. As U.S. State Department deputy spokesman Adam Ereli put it with a valid sense of triumph, "The United States opposes any unilateral change from the status quo."

Imagine the panic that would have been caused in the State Department if an order had been made for the new year that the phrases "unilateral change" and "status quo" were to be struck from further use within the department. There would be no choice but to cancel all future press conferences and public statements.

Maybe it would even call for the cancellation of the State Department.

But none of that happened. Something did happen, however, that indicated a victory for business and a defeat for political principle that President Chen had outlined in his strong New Year's Resolution Speech. The year 2006 brought a membership application to the World Semiconductor Council (WSC) from the People's Republic of China. Immediately the WSC changed the name of its member, Taiwan, to Chinese Taipei. This was an opportunity for President Chen to reject such appeasement and to display that giving in to such faulty national designation was not worth the economic gain of being in the council and, therefore, submit a resignation from the World Semiconductor Council. He did not submit a resignation. Chinese Taipei is now the official designation listed by the WSC.

Beyond those incidents, something else dominated the news of Taiwan, and this news would increase the popularity of Chairman Ma as the chief opposition figure to President Chen. What happened had nothing to do with the policies of either of the two men, but rather it was an escalation of the pre-election scandal that had enveloped the president. Political scandals rarely get better as time goes by; they usually get worse, and the charges against President Chen got very much worse. By the end of June 2006 he was smothered with charges; none directed at him personally, but there were serious charges leveled against Chen family members. His son-in-law was detained with a charge of insider trading while President Chen's wife was charged with accepting gift vouchers from Sogo Department Store in return for giving help to a businessman regarding Sogo's ownership. The charges were denied by his son-in-law and by the first lady, but all of this had a devastating effect on President Chen. The scandal caused President Chen to relinquish most domestic policy decisions to Premier Su Tseng-chang, allowing Premier Su to make any nominations for cabinet changes he wanted as well as having complete responsibility for all cabinet policies.

President Chen's approval ratings dropped to a new low. Pro-Chen and anti-Chen demonstrations were held with frequency. Major speakers at anti-Chen demonstrations were Pan-Blue party officials.

On June 27, 2006, Taiwan's legislature, the Legislative Yuan, took a vote on a motion to recall President Chen from office. A recall could be achieved only if it received a two-thirds majority. The recall failed, receiving 119 votes out of the 221 members of the Legislative Yuan on that date.

Chairman Ma said that the Democratic Progressive Party legislators had chosen to "stand side by side with corruption." The Kuomintang pledged to continue to have him removed, this time by a signature campaign urging President Chen to resign.

During the end of the summer of 2006, the campaign for his resignation ignited into daily demonstrations led by a former chairman of President Chen's Democratic Progressive Party, Shih Ming-teh. Along with the demonstrations, which were attended most heavily by the Kuomintang Party, came the allegation that President Chen was himself corrupt and responsible for undocumented use of state funds.

The scandal delighted those who wanted the Kuomintang to win the 2008 election. Therefore, it delighted the Kuomintang, it delighted the U.S. State Department, and it delighted President Hu Jintao of the People's Republic of China.

CHAPTER TWENTY

THE POLICY OF POSTPONEMENT

THE UNITED STATES has long had a Policy of Postponement regarding China's threat to Taiwan, and even a Policy of Postponement regarding China's potential of becoming a superpower hostile to the United States while that potential has continued to enlarge. It would not be far-fetched to recognize the possibility of China and Russia forming a partnership and, in addition, having some temporary allies from the European Union. Happily, EU members are democracies and those who might choose a partnership with China can only last as long as the people of their countries want their leadership. There is, however, no guarantee that those who follow would be better. Unfortunately, just as in the United States, many businesspeople of the EU have a greater interest in exporting products and importing banknotes than they have for the human rights of others.

Near the end of the 1980s and the beginning of the 1990s, three of the most significant events occurred in China and Taiwan since the 1949 takeover of China by Mao Tse-tung and the defeated government going to Taiwan. One of the events took place in China; two of the events took place in Taiwan. But the United States maintains the same (or worse) policies we observed prior to those events.

The event in China was the Tiananmen Square Massacre—but we are closer to China now than we were prior to the Tiananmen Square Massacre.

The events in Taiwan were the adoption of a full democracy as its system, and second, its renunciation of any claim to China. That left the name of their country; the Republic of China, to be both anachronistic and totally inaccurate. Therefore, there has been a strong movement of Taiwanese to be realistic. They want to change the name from the Republic of *China* because they know and admit it is *not* the Republic of China.

U.S. policy, however, insists they retain that antiquated name. Why do we retain such a demand that ignores the facts? The State Department authored that continuing demand because of the *People's* Republic of China's insistence there should be no change. If the name was changed to the Republic of Taiwan rather than the Republic of China, the People's Republic of China would have no case in insisting on a "one China" policy for the nations of the world—including ours. When Taiwan became a democracy and gave up its claim of China, which should have been a cause for congratulating Taiwan in conceding to realism, it became a cause for a PRC policy of deception and a U.S. Policy of Postponement in dealing with the truth.

With the Anti-Secession Law passed by the National People's Congress of the People's Republic of China making a very loud and unambiguous warning of possible "non-peaceful means" to take over Taiwan, the U.S. Policy of Postponement could enter a new and more dangerous phase if China and the rest of the world believes the United States is willing to *continue* that postponement no matter the PRC's cross-strait warnings.

To be precise on our current policy, we maintain a "one China" policy, and Taiwan is part of China, the legal government of China is the People's Republic of China, and we want a resolution to come about peacefully while both sides maintain the status quo."

What?

What the devil does that mean? For sure, anyone can understand the call for a *temporary* status quo since we have enough on our plate. There should be no argument that the United States must win the war against Islamist terrorism. Therefore, for the duration of the war it is preferable for a status quo to be maintained among foreign powers in conflicts that could divert the U.S. military from their immediate goal. But to ignore such extreme changes in the status quo by the People's Republic of China that could endanger the United States at China's timing makes a travesty of our China-Taiwan policy. Moreover, there should be no maintenance of the myth that the government of the People's Republic of China has any intention of halting its help to rogue regimes including Iran, North Korea, Sudan, and Myanmar (Burma).

> It was the status quo of the Middle East that led to the bombing of our embassies in Kenya and Tanzania. It was the status quo in the Middle East that led to the attack of the U.S.S. *Cole* that killed 17 American sailors. It was the status quo in the Middle East that produced 19 hijackers and took planes and crashed them into the Pentagon and the World Trade Towers, and killed nearly 3,000 innocent people on September 11, 2001. The status quo in the Middle East was dangerous and unacceptable, and our security demanded that we change it. Secondly, the idea that lasting stability can be achieved by denying people a voice in the future control of their destiny is wrong.

Those are the words of President George W. Bush to the American Legion on February 24, 2006.

That statement of the president regarding the Middle East is totally valid. Its validity could someday be moved eastward. There are great threats presented by China to both the immediate goal of defeating Islamist terrorism and to the longer-range pursuit of achieving liberty for all the peoples of the world. We cannot ignore that a key threat is pointed at Taiwan, made fragile by its well armed and threatening enemy as we demand a status quo and continue to pretend that *anyone* of *any* influence is claiming there should be a *"two China"* policy, as had been the case many years ago.

Somewhere, sometime in the international arena it should be candidly admitted that there was a deliberate State Department misinterpretation given to the Shanghai Communiqué, and that misinterpretation served as the basis for the forthcoming Carter and Reagan communiqués. That is important to do because surely the PRC will continue to say we must abide by those three communiqués, the latter two stating that the People's Republic of China is the legal government of China and Taiwan is part of it. Even *more important* in the world of diplomacy where every word has a meaning vivisected under magnifying glasses, the nations of the world should be reminded that all three communiqués were written prior to the late 1980s before Taiwan *became* a democracy and *before* it *renounced* its claim of wanting to have jurisdiction of China, while the People's Republic of China retains its one-party, non-elected dictatorial system of government, continues to justify its abhorrent human rights policies, and demands jurisdiction over Taiwan.

There are those in D.C. who shake their heads and hold to the old policies regarding China and Taiwan when circumstances were different. One of the new circumstances is the multiplication of the military of the People's Republic of China. D.C. is full of voices saying, "The People's Republic of China has no plans to attack Taiwan; China's leaders are too interested in economic progress, and China does not want to risk its new place of prestige on the world stage, particularly when it is scheduled to host the 2008 Olympic Games."

Maybe they are right about China's leaders not risking the prestige they seek in the hosting of the Olympic Games; it is certainly a logical conclusion, but we can never count on tyrannies using *our* logic to determine *their* actions. In the late 1970s it was thought by top U.S. policy makers, including President Carter, that aggression of the Soviet Union would decline or at least be contained because the Soviet Union was scheduled to host the 1980 Olympic Games in Moscow. Less than seven months before the Olympic Games began, to the surprise of U.S. policy makers, the Soviet Union invaded Afghanistan. President Carter admitted, "My opinion of the Russians has changed more drastically in the last week than even the previous two and a half years."

In 1989 it was assumed by our top policy makers that the People's Republic of China would not crack down on the demonstrators in Tiananmen Square. "One million people are in the square with the world media watching. Gorbachev will be in Beijing. Dan Rather is already there. They wouldn't dare crack down." But they did.

U.S. Secretary of State Condoleezza Rice wisely said, "We are concerned about the military balance and have said to China that they should do nothing militarily to provoke Taiwan."

Deputy Secretary of State Robert Zoellick picked up on the attitude coming from above and said we warned the EU not to end their embargo of technology and weapons to China: "If there ever were a point where there were some conflict or danger and European equipment helped kill American men and women in conflict, that would not be good for the relationship."

In June 2005, State Department Spokesman Sean McCormack had said: "Sixteen years after the brutal and tragic events of Tiananmen Square, we still remember the many Chinese citizens killed, detained, or missing in connection with the protests. Besides those who died, thousands of Chinese were arrested and sentenced without trial, and as many as 250 still languish in prison for Tiananmen-related activities. We call on the Chinese government to fully account for the thousands killed, detained, or missing, and to release those unjustly imprisoned. Moreover, family members of victims, like the Tiananmen mothers, and other citizens who urge their government to undertake a reassessment of what happened June 4, 1989, should be free from harassment and detention. It is now time for the Chinese government to move forward with a re-examination of Tiananmen, and give its citizens the ability to flourish by allowing them to think, speak, assemble, and worship freely. We continue to urge China to bring its human rights practices into conformity with international standards and law."

Most important of all was a statement Secretary of State Rice made in Cairo on June 25, 2005: "For 60 years my country, the United States, pursued stability at the expense of democracy in this region, here in the Middle East, and we achieved neither. ["We" undoubtedly meant the State Department.] Now we are taking a different course. We are supporting the democratic aspirations of all people."

With all the positive, clear statements of principle, there arose a disturbing contrast between what President George W. Bush answered to the same question on April 25, 2001, and, after being in office over four years, on June 8, 2005. Both times he was asked, with small variation, the same question. As recorded here in Chapter 1, on April 25, 2001, ABC's Charlie Gibson asked the president: "I'm curious if you, in your own mind, feel that if Taiwan were attacked by China, do we have an obligation to defend the Taiwanese?"

"Yes we do," the president answered. "And the Chinese must understand that. Yes, I would."

"With the full force of the American military?"

"Whatever it took to help Taiwan defend theirself."

That was clear and definitive. And that was that.

On June 8, 2005, Neil Cavuto of the Fox News Channel asked President Bush, "Do we still stand by an agreement, Mr. President, that if Taiwan is ever invaded, we will defend Taiwan?"

"Yes, we do." [The first three words were the same as 2001 but four years after that 2001 interview, his answer expanded into State Department–trained ambiguity.] "Yes, we do. It's called the Taiwan Relations Act. The policy of the U.S. government is this: We're for a 'one China' policy based upon what they call the Three Communiqués, and that we adhere to the Taiwan Relations Act, which means this: neither side will unilaterally change the status quo. In other words, neither side will make a decision that steps outside the bounds of that statement I just made to you. If China were to invade unilaterally, we would rise up in the spirit of [the] Taiwan Relations Act. If Taiwan were to declare independence unilaterally, it would be a unilateral decision that would then change the U.S. equation. My attitude is that time will heal this issue. And therefore we're trying to make sure that neither side provokes the other through unilateral action."

Neither side? By consistently talking about "neither side" we are side-stepping the fact that the government of China is a dictatorship and Taiwan is a democracy. A "'one China' policy based upon what they call the Three Communiqués" certainly suggests that as long as there is no attack on Taiwan by China, that we endorse Beijing having jurisdiction over Taiwan. How could it mean anything else?

The epitome of contrast in the White House treatment of China and Taiwan occurred in the spring of 2006. On April 20, President Hu Jintao of China was greeted on the South Lawn of the White House by President Bush with both presidents giving speeches, the playing of China's national anthem, and President Hu given a twenty-one-gun salute. The following month, President Chen of Taiwan was traveling to Latin America and requested a refueling and rest stop in either New York or San Francisco. Neither stop was permitted by the U.S. State Department, rejecting any transit point within the conterminous area of the United States. He was, instead, offered a refueling stop in either Alaska or Hawaii, as long as his presence was kept only at the airport with no overnight stay. President Chen rejected the rather humiliating offer.

On June 28, 2006, the U.S. House of Representatives adopted a measure (through an amendment to a funding bill for the State Department and other government entities) that would prevent any spending on banning Taiwan officials from the White House and the State Department, and prevent any prohibitions of U.S. officials attending Taiwan National Day celebrations, prevent any prohibitions of senior military officials from visiting Taiwan, and prohibit funding on other prohibitions between the United States and Taiwan, including how to compose a "thank-you" note to officials from Taiwan. The vote on the funding bill to which the amendment was attached was 393 to 23.

The effort was led by representatives from both major political parties: Robert Andrews, Sherrod Brown, Steve Chabot, Dana Rohrabacher, and others. Another long-time supporter of Taiwan, Representative Thomas Tancredo, spoke in support of the amendment, saying the old guidelines to be prohibited "needlessly complicate our ability to effectively communicate with our friends in Taiwan." Congressman Frank Wolf added, "There are forty Catholic bishops and priests in jail in China and zero in jail in Taiwan."

Jiang Yu, spokesperson for the Chinese Foreign Ministry, said, "Approving this draft bill is a serious violation of the fundamental principles of bilateral relations" and that it was contrary to the "one China" policy of the United States.

The U.S. State Department agreed with Jiang Yu and not with the U.S. House of Representatives. A senior State Department official announced: "The administration is opposed to this measure because it interferes with the president's prerogative to conduct our foreign relations."

One of the great incompatibilities of U.S. foreign policy, authored and consistently encouraged by the State Department to administrations of both major parties, is that while we insist on a "one state" ("one China") solution to the conflict between Taiwan and China, we insist on a "two state" solution to the conflict between Israel and the Palestinian Authority. Why is Taiwan *not* entitled to a state of its own while the Palestinian Authority *is* entitled to a state of its own? Making the contradictory policies more incoherent is that while Taiwan has no ambition to take over China, much of the Palestinian Authority has the admitted ambition to take over Israel. And while Taiwan is pro–United States, much of the Palestinian Authority is adamantly opposed to the United States.

Right or wrong, there was a time when a "one China" policy made some sense. After all, during those days there were two separate political and geographical entities, each one with a leader saying, "I represent the legal government of China." A "one China" policy meant we could only recognize one of those two entities as China's legal government, which is why the policy became known as a "one China" policy. But on May 1, 1991, the leader of Taiwan, President Lee, *formally* ended the advocacy of the Kuomintang government's 1949 pledge to rule China. (In fact, it was *informally* known long before then.) There is not one political power of any credibility in Taiwan that calls for Taiwan to be the legal government of China. So, of course, we believe in one China. That's all there is. But whether or not Taiwan is *part* of China is a different issue. China still wants to take over Taiwan, even by force or "non-peaceful means" as China puts it, while Taiwan simply wants to be Taiwan. By the United States and other nations holding to the vocabulary of the past, the policy complicates what has been a very simple reality since at least 1991. It is no less than outrageous that the United States government opposes Taiwan removing from its constitution that it is the legal government of China (because it would change the status quo).

With the hope that someday we replace that policy statement that has no logical reason for being maintained, we could then get to a reasonable assessment of the question of whether or not Taiwan should be part of China.

Most people on Taiwan are not Chinese. Many of them are surely descendants of Chinese, but even those Chinese who came to Taiwan as recently as 1949 with Chiang Kai-shek are now a couple generations back, and their children and grandchildren are Taiwanese, joining the majority of the population whose Chinese ancestors go even further back or have no Chinese background at all, and some who are aboriginals. Similarly, most Americans have descendants that were not Americans, but do they want the country of their grandparents, or even further back, to be the country with whom they "unite"—and have that foreign government as their own government, rather than the United States? Our policy does not indicate opposition to that kind of transfer of sovereignty for the people of Taiwan.

Compare China with Great Britain: Throughout most of the first half of the twentieth century there was a British Empire of sixty-two colonies and forty-five other political entities, including dominions, protectorates, associated states, as well as mandated and trust territories. It was a common occurrence to be reminded of the international expression "the sun never sets on the British Empire," and it didn't. Now it does. It sets on Great Britain every day. With the exception of small islands that have consistently *chosen* to remain British protectorates, the rest have been given independence. All of them could have been labeled by Great Britain as "renegade provinces, for which non-peaceful means and other protective measures to protect Great Britain's sovereignty and territorial integrity will be employed should they declare independence." But the respect of *people* rather than lust for territory by the leadership of Great Britain is in direct contrast to the leadership of the People's Republic of China's lust for territory along with their *dis*respect shown to people. Add to that the fact that the government of the People's Republic of China has *never* ruled Taiwan.

Ambiguity should be taken down from its revered place in diplomacy. It can create misunderstandings of our position by the threatening party. During the Cuban Missile Crisis of October 1962, President Kennedy thrust aside all measures of ambiguity, saying, "If any nuclear missile is launched *from Cuba* against *any nation in the Western Hemisphere*, this nation will regard it as an attack *by the Soviet Union* on the *United States*."

The world is going through a unique and magnificent period of history. In President George W. Bush's second inaugural address and in his 2005 State of the Union address he embarked upon the grandest pursuit of mankind: for everyone in the world to be free from smothering governments who steal people's God-given birthright—liberty.

In this young century alone, Americans have died to bring about democracies in Afghanistan and Iraq where elections have now taken place, and Americans continue to die for liberty. It would be the epitome of ironic tragedy for Taiwan, already a democracy, to be taken over by a government that rejects liberty.

While the United States so admirably worked toward and praised Iraq for holding a referendum for their democratically oriented constitution on October 15, 2005, the policy of the United States opposes a referendum for a democratically oriented constitution in Taiwan.

If Taiwan's democracy is considered to be expendable to gain the favor of the People's Republic of China, oppression will be the victor and democracy will be the loser well beyond Taiwan. Other nations would not only witness the takeover of a free people, but that chapter of our times would give encouragement to other dictators of the world, enhancing their belief that liberty is simply a fanciful vision of those they despise.

The people of Taiwan live in near diplomatic isolation because most Taiwanese, at least so far, have chosen principle to appeasement, democracy to dictatorship, and independence to servitude. Over two centuries ago, we in the United States had Founders who held to the same convictions. The only difference is that Taiwan is struggling not to achieve liberty. It already has it. As a threatened democracy, Taiwan's struggle is to retain the liberty it has achieved.

The rest of the world could prove its sense of morality by allowing a new name to enter the intricate glossary of national sovereignty and international relations: the Republic of Taiwan.

INDEX